Exploring
Critical Issues
in Gifted Education

Exploring Critical Issues
in Gifted Education

Christine L. Weber, Ph.D.,
Cecilia Boswell, Ed.D., and
Wendy A. Behrens, M.A. Ed.

Copublished With the

NATIONAL ASSOCIATION FOR
Gifted Children

PRUFROCK PRESS INC.
WACO, TEXAS

Library of Congress Cataloging-in-Publication Data

Weber, Christine L.
 Exploring critical issues in gifted education : a case studies approach / by Christine L. Weber, Ph.D.,
Cecilia Boswell, Ed.D., and Wendy A. Behrens.
   pages cm
 ISBN 978-1-61821-097-5 (pbk.)
 1. Gifted children--Education--Case studies. 2. Gifted children--Education--Standards--United
States. 3. Curriculum planning--United States. I. Title.
 LC3993.W37 2013
 371.95--dc23
                        2013019014

Edited by Rachel Taliaferro

Cover design by Raquel Trevino and layout design by Allegra Denbo

ISBN-13: 978-1-61821-097-5

Printed in the United States of America.

At the time of this book's publication, all facts and figures cited are the most current available. All telephone numbers, addresses, and websites URLs are accurate and active. All publications, organizations,
websites, and other resources exist as described in the book, and all have been verified. The authors and
Prufrock Press Inc. make no warranty or guarantee concerning the information and materials given out
by organizations or content found at websites, and we are not responsible for any changes that occur
after this book's publication. If you find an error, please contact Prufrock Press Inc.

Prufrock Press Inc.
P.O. Box 8813
Waco, TX 76714-8813
Phone: (800) 998-2208
Fax: (800) 240-0333
http://www.prufrock.com

Table of Contents

Acknowledgments

———◦◦◦———

Thank you to the administrators, teachers, counselors, parents, and students who inspired our case studies. We particularly wish to recognize Dr. Susan K. Johnsen for her reflections on the value of case studies in professional development. We also extend a special thank you to graduate assistant Amanda Laukitis for her tireless and meticulous editing of our work.

Foreword

I am pleased to provide some initial reflections about this new book that focuses on using case studies in professional development to implement the National Association for Gifted Children's (NAGC) Pre-K–Grade 12 Gifted Programming Standards. The standards that are aligned to the case studies in this volume are part of a wider network of professional standards that influence the education of all students. Therefore, in addressing the Programming Standards, the authors have also addressed the NAGC/Council for Exceptional Children, The Association for the Gifted (CEC-TAG; 2006) teacher preparation standards, the Interstate Teacher Assessment and Support Consortium (InTASC) standards (Council of Chief State School Officers [CCSSO], 2011), and the National Board for Professional Teaching Standards (NBPTS, 2011) because they are all closely aligned. This information is important to those who may be using these case studies with different audiences in general, gifted, and special education settings.

Using the Programming Standards as guidelines for professional development, the authors have addressed the full gamut of knowledge and skills from characteristics of gifted and talented students to programming and professional development. In this way, the participants not only have opportunities to apply their prior understandings but also learn about evidence-based practices that are important to implement. The case studies therefore provide the structure for identifying best practices and become critical points of departure for discussing policies, rules, procedures, and classroom instructional practices.

The authors also incorporate the 2011 Standards for Professional Learning from the National Staff Development Council. These standards emphasize the importance of educator participation in learning communities where they take an active role in learning new information. This approach is emphasized throughout the book where participants have opportunities to discuss the data presented in the case and select activities and extensions that are relevant to their situation. All of the cases and activities have a strong research base as demonstrated by the extensive references that include theory, models, and evidence-based practices.

The professional development leader is armed with instructional strategies for using the cases. These incorporate the higher level thinking processes of problem solving and decision making. The scenario presented in each case lends itself to the problem-based learning process. Leaders who use these strategies will be able to provide a model that educators can immediately transfer to their classrooms.

The cases are quite varied and will be engaging to a wide range of users. Some cases are useful for those without an extensive background in gifted education because more information is provided in the presentation of the case, and the discussion questions focus on characteristics of gifted students and more basic issues, such as parenting and services within general education settings (see cases "James" and "Ingrid"). Other cases require more prerequisite information, such as "Claire," where participants need to modify the Response to Intervention (RtI) pyramid to include gifted and advanced students, and "Eric," where participants need to evaluate an identification profile, interpret scores, and design assessments.

Cases also vary by grade level, role, and school setting. For example, the "Mike, Martha, and Lucy" case provides data for decision making at secondary levels, whereas the "Mrs. Lewis" case is about a second-through-fifth-grade resource teacher. Parents might enjoy the "Jessica" and "Ingrid" cases because of the parents' perspectives presented in the scenario, while administrators might appreciate the "Lenore School District" and "Dumont Public School District" cases. These latter scenarios present problems related to the provision of services with limited resources and the creation of nonbiased, equitable assessment procedures in a highly diverse school district. In addition, the school context varies with some cases occurring in rural settings (see "Mrs. Lewis") and others in urban settings (see "STARS"); some in public (see "Mike, Martha, and Lucy") and others in private schools (see "Henderson Day School"); and some in small schools (see "James"); and others in large schools (see "Dumont Public School District"). This variation will be particularly useful for differentiating the content of the workshop, seminar, or class for the participants.

The authors need to be commended for their inclusion of a wide range of students from diverse backgrounds. For example, "Jessica," has a learning disability in reading but is also gifted in the arts. "Raul" and "Eric" present some of the issues in working with students who are from minority groups or who are English language learners. Urban and rural districts with minority populations are also represented in the scenarios, such as "Skylar School District" and "Dumont Public School District." Participants need to grapple with the challenges associated with providing equal access and services to these underrepresented, at-risk populations.

As the authors suggest, using web-based resources and reflective journaling might enhance the cases. It would also be helpful, particularly in addressing more complex cases, for participants to read some of the background information prior to addressing the issues presented in the scenario. In this way, the discussion will be based on more evidence-based practices, which are provided by the authors in resource sections. Overall, I found the cases to be realistic and based on situations that are familiar to those of us who have worked in gifted education. They examine important topics to the field and should be useful not only in Pre-K through grade 12 settings but also at the university level. I look forward to using them myself in my classes. I congratulate the authors on a practical resource that will be useful in myriad professional development opportunities.

—Susan K. Johnsen, Ph.D.
Professor, Department of Educational Psychology, Baylor University

Introduction

◆◈◈◈◆

Why Read a Book on Case Studies
for Professional Development?

Although the best way to provide opportunities for educators to analyze and reflect on various situations in education is through field experiences and hands-on practice, it is not always easy or even possible to organize such encounters with experienced professionals, especially in the field of gifted education. Burkman's (2012) study, related to preparing novice teachers for success in elementary classrooms, identified teaching gifted and talented students in the top 25% of the list of challenges faced in the classroom. It is important to note these novice teachers also ranked interactive and cooperative learning as a method of presentation that would be most meaningful or appealing for the delivery of professional development. Thus, we need to take into consideration how to provide the best training and instruction for educators and stakeholders working with gifted and talented students. In order to better prepare educators and other school personnel to work with these children, we have developed a book of case studies representing various problem-based learning scenarios that focus on information and authentic stories gathered from our own experiences. These encounters range from those exemplified by teachers, parents, administrators, higher education professionals, and state leaders, with each representing events that occur in elementary, middle, and high school classrooms located in a variety of settings. We find that learning scenarios have enormous appeal and are appropriate for professional development because they:

- can be read and discussed in a short amount of time;
- allow the reader to gain greater understanding through empathy;

- encourage an active response;
- encourage an analysis of multiple perspectives;
- illustrate active problem-solving strategies that can be modeled and used with participants;
- encourage reflection on various solutions, thereby opening doors to new possibilities; and
- provide resources for further exploration of issues related to the case.

We have also discovered that learning scenarios mirroring real-world problems that end in a dilemma engage the reader in a reflective analysis of teaching and learning. This book portrays learning scenario *narratives*, each with brief *introductions* that provide an overview of the case before proceeding to read the entire scenario. Within each case, the *things to consider* section supplies the reader with essential information without imparting an explicit action, recommendation, or solution. *Discussion questions, activities, extensions,* and *suggestions for further reading* support the standards of excellence set forth in the revised *NAGC Pre-K–Grade 12 Gifted Education Programming Standards* (2010; see Appendix A). It is our goal that educators draw from the cases presented, which situate learning in authentic and meaningful contexts for the purpose of improving the identification of and services for gifted and talented students in light of these new standards. There are several decision-making strategies provided that one could use during various stages of analysis to enhance the understanding of each learning scenario.

What Will You Learn From Case Studies?

The learning scenarios encourage a detailed analysis and critical reflection of the most current and prevalent issues in gifted education, such as identifying gifted children of poverty, differentiating instruction, implementing grouping practices, meeting social and emotional needs, serving twice-exceptional students, incorporating Response to Intervention (RtI), and facing the reality of limited resources. These scenarios constitute real-life experiences of the authors representing those dilemmas typically found in schools. It should be noted that all names have been changed in an effort to preserve the privacy of the individuals, schools, and communities portrayed in the case studies. In some cases, the attributes of several students have been combined to illustrate the complexity of student needs.

This book offers the opportunity for educators and stakeholders to examine giftedness in a variety of contexts that are authentic in nature. It is recommended that readers work in pairs or in small groups to investigate and analyze the scenarios using a five-step model adapted from the work of Finkle and Torp's (1995) problem-based learning, as further developed in Chapter 1. Each case supports an examination of one of the *NAGC Pre-K–Grade 12 Gifted Education Programming Standards* (2010), which includes:

- Standard 1: Learning and Development
- Standard 2: Assessment
- Standard 3: Curriculum Planning & Instruction
- Standard 4: Learning Environments
- Standard 5: Programming
- Standard 6: Professional Development

Who Might Benefit From Analyzing the Cases?

Case studies provide an opportunity for both the prospective teacher and in-service teacher to begin anticipating the issues that they might encounter and be required to resolve. Specifically, those who would benefit include:

- Preservice teachers enrolled in general and special education coursework.
- In-service teachers enrolled in advanced and/or graduate level coursework.
- All educators (teachers, administrators, counselors, psychologists, support staff) enrolled in gifted and talented endorsement, certification, and/or professional development coursework.
- Practitioners at any level of professional development, responding to cases through discussion, who may refine understanding, explore more in-depth, reflect on current practices, and extend his or her perspective.
- Parents and community members who wish to learn more about students who are gifted and talented.

How Will Reading Case Studies Be Relevant to Your Educational Practice?

We have discovered that the approach of presenting issues in a case study related to educating gifted and talented learners influences both the classroom and school setting by:

- requiring connection to formal learning with real-life situations;
- relying on personal experiences to collect, interpret, and explain circumstances presented in the case;
- providing facts and limitations related to a particular event;
- encouraging the examination of possible interpretations;
- using inquiry to investigate what is happening; and

- requiring reflection of a situation for learning, while providing different perspectives on common problems.

This knowledge base and set of skills are essential for making effective decisions related to meeting the needs of gifted learners, whether you are a parent, educator, administrator, counselor, or other school personnel. Kuntz and Hessler (1998) stated that the case study method effectively enhances learning because it:

- develops higher order thinking skills;
- illustrates the relevance of the study in society;
- asks readers to question assumptions underlying the theories presented; and
- most importantly, exhibits learning from the cases long after the study concludes (pp. 7–9).

How Does Our Case Study Book Differ From Others?

Each learning scenario is specifically designed to help the reader explore critical issues within the field and includes the following components:

- addresses an important issue in educating gifted and talented children;
- engages the readers in the study of a variety of issues from a pedagogical and conceptual perspective;
- presents a dilemma commonly found in the field and provides decision-making tools to facilitate inquiry and stimulate an interactive response;
- is open-ended, providing motivating "what if" questions for further study of the issue;
- provides an opportunity for analysis implementing the NAGC Programming Standards (2010); and
- supports professional development opportunities for all educators and stakeholders involved in the education of gifted learners.

The matrix on page 17 represents the cases and their key issues provided for discussion and analysis in this book. The *NAGC Pre-K–Grade 12 Gifted Education Programming Standards* (2010) align with each case.

A Matrix of Case Studies

	Title	Key Issue(s)	
Chapter 2	Claire	Response to Intervention (RtI)	**Standard 1: Learning and Development**
	Wyatt	Identification, characteristics, and middle school issues	
	Jessica	Characteristics of twice-exceptional learners	
Chapter 3	Eric	Assessing programs and evaluating services	**Standard 2: Assessment**
	Dumont Public Schools	Assessing students for services	
	Tonya	Identifying creatively gifted students	
Chapter 4	Mrs. Lewis	Curriculum and differentiated instruction in rural schools	**Standard 3: Curriculum Planning & Instruction**
	Mr. Jackson and Miss Mendoza	Tiered assignments	
	Mike, Martha, and Lucy	Analysis of data to inform instruction appropriately	
Chapter 5	Raul	Special populations, at-risk learners, and cultural competency	**Standard 4: Learning Environments**
	Rebecca	Special populations	
	Ingrid	Social-emotional; parent's view	
Chapter 6	Lenore School District	Program services in rural schools	**Standard 5: Programming**
	Martin	Acceleration	
	Skylar School District	Defensible programs	
	STARS	Services in the middle school years	
	Avery, Ethan, and Brazos	Young gifted with varying needs	
Chapter 7	Rosamaria	Professional development; counteracting bias	**Standard 6: Professional Development**
	Hendersonville Day School	Professional development for implementing differentiation	
	University School District	Professional development related to creating classrooms for gifted and advanced learners	

Finally, tools for analysis and decision-making are provided in Appendix B to help examine all of the nuances presented in the scenario without missing key points and critical ideas.

Chapter 1

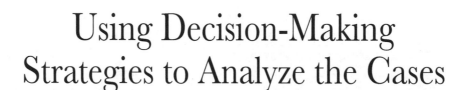

Using Decision-Making Strategies to Analyze the Cases

What Are the Components of the Problem-Based Case Study and How Will They Be Used?

The learning scenario presented in each case study provides an introduction, followed by a detailed narrative of a particular problem or set of issues within a dilemma related to educating gifted and talented students. Each scenario narrative encourages reflection on the key issue or issues. Using an organizer process from problem-based learning, adapted from the work of Finkle and Torp (1995) and discussed later in the chapter, the reader can begin to make decisions related to planning a course of action.

The Things to Consider portion of each case provides the reader with essential information for careful consideration before making a decision. Suggested steps for "solving" a problem-based learning scenario are included and are typical of the "who, what, when, where, why, and to what extent" process taught to classroom students.

The case studies encourage discussion and can be used in a variety of settings. They offer opportunities for role-playing different parts in the scenario and promote interviewing. When only a portion of the case is presented, readers may "interview" another student or the instructor to extract information. Written or take-home assignments are provided as well. It is important that the *NAGC Pre-K–Grade 12 Programming Standards* be considered when making decisions about implementing high quality services for gifted learners. The discussion questions, activities, and extensions encourage the reader to consider the impact of these standards on the case presented.

Discussion questions specifically encourage exploration of the issue or issues presented in the learning scenario. They encourage the reflection of personal and professional philosophies and may stimulate further investigations provided in the activities that follow. It is crucial that these questions be used to guide the direction of the discussion. A variety of questions particular to the case are provided allowing the facilitator or reader to choose to answer some or all of them, before proceeding to the activities and extensions. Although it is critical to maintain the integrity of a dilemma with various solutions possible, the reader or group must recognize that some solutions are more easily implemented or probable in given situations. Allowing adequate time to examine these questions helps to ensure that different perspectives and viewpoints are considered. Although discussion questions particular to each case are included, a series of generic questions should also be considered. Stepien and Gallagher (1993) identified metacognitive questions; for instance: What is going on here? What do we need to know more about? What was done during the problem that was effective? The following list includes additional generic questions to consider:

- Who is the focus of the case study?
- What is the primary issue to be addressed?
- Is there a secondary issue?
- What cultural factors impact this case study (e.g., socioeconomic status, limited language proficiency, ethnicity, traditions, values/beliefs, family setting, community norms)?
- What other factors are relevant to the case study (e.g., evidence of special abilities, mental and physical health limitations or concerns, safety, learning differences, learning style, access to services, motivation, engagement, achievement)?
- With whom could you collaborate to resolve the issue(s)?
- What course of action would you recommend?
- What research supports your recommendation?
- What additional information or resources would be helpful?

Use of such questions encourages the reader to take responsibility for the problem. Over a period of time, self-directed learning is encouraged and there is less scaffolding needed. Activities prompt further exploration of the issues involved in the case, while extensions provide an opportunity for the reader to apply understanding and insights related to the issue presented in another context, field, or situation. These extensions often provide an opportunity to generalize beyond the particular case. Choosing to participate in one or more of the activities and/or extensions ensures that insight into the topic is obtained. Suggestions for further reading offer the facilitator and/or reader additional resources to broaden the concept for enhanced understanding.

A case study matrix found in the beginning of the book represents the various topics and *NAGC Pre-K–Grade 12 Gifted Education Programming Standards* (2010), supported within each case. This is especially helpful in selecting a case to meet a specific professional development or training need.

What Are the Steps in a Case Study Analysis? How Can Decision-Making Strategies Help Enhance the Analysis?

Cases are best analyzed by working in pairs or small groups. This helps to maximize the discussion and to support various insights from differing perspectives. In order to gain the greatest benefit in a professional development setting, it may be helpful to identify a facilitator who is not only knowledgeable about issues related to educating gifted learners, but is able to support the group by modeling the problem-solving and decision-making processes. It is helpful for the facilitator to clarify that problem solving deals with gathering and sorting facts in order to analyze the issues in a systematic way. Decision making requires that choices be made at each step of problem solving, thus leading to actions. The following steps, and problem-solving and decision-making strategies, reinforce the problem-based learning process (adapted from the work of Finkle & Torp, 1995) and are suggested when considering solutions for the learning scenario.

1. The problem is read and reviewed and the facts are identified.
2. A discussion based on the facts occurs.
3. Broad problem results are identified.
4. Determination is made of what is needed (resources) in order to gather information.
5. Possible actions, recommendations, or solutions are analyzed and presented.

Begin by understanding the case. Read the scenario carefully. Focus on the key facts that would influence comprehension of the issue(s). Be sure to identify the Six Ws: who, what, when, where, why, and to what extent in the discussion (see Figure 1 and Appendix B). Consider role modeling various perspectives of the different stakeholders. Answering the generic questions previously presented in this chapter may also be helpful at this point.

A Hexagonal Radial (see Figure 2 and Appendix B) can also provide a more in-depth overview of a case study for further understanding including questions such as what happened, where did it happen, why did it happen, etc. A simple chart (see Figure 3 and Appendix B) can also be used to begin to explore the

Who	
What	
Where	
When	
Why	
To What Extent	

Figure 1. Six Ws.

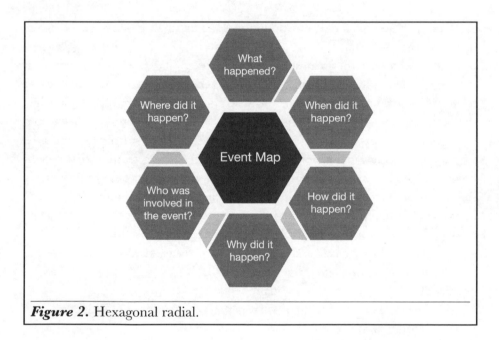

Figure 2. Hexagonal radial.

facts presented, including the focus, issues, and factors including cultural factors. Another tool for helping to understand the facts of a case is a Basic Radial (see Figure 4 and Appendix B), which considers the following factors: additional information/research, supporting documents, collaborations, and course of action for a case.

Answer the suggested questions for the case. Many of the questions require the *NAGC Pre-K–Grade 12 Gifted Education Programming Standards* to be taken into consideration and to reflect on how they might impact the decision-making process. List any other questions concerning the case. Record what is found interesting. Respond to questions posed if possible. Some questions may remain unanswered. A T-chart, represented in Figure 5 is helpful in recording questions and responses (see Appendix B).

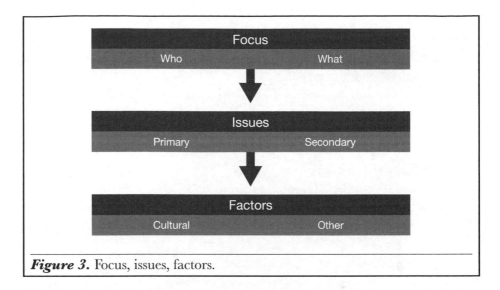

Figure 3. Focus, issues, factors.

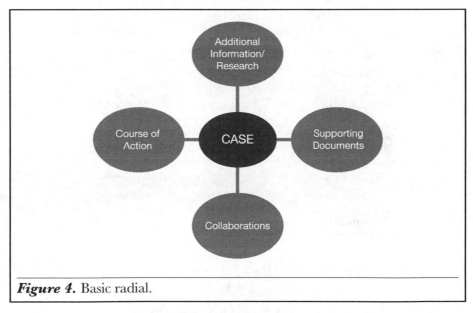

Figure 4. Basic radial.

QUESTIONS	RESPONSES

Figure 5. T-chart.

After summarizing the key facts, try to narrow down a possible issue(s) or problem(s). Be sure to consider other factors (e.g., cultural, economic, pedagogical) that might influence the events in the scenario. If necessary, discuss resources needed to help further the analysis.

One problem-solving strategy (see Figure 6 and Appendix B) identified by Swartz and Parks (1994), incorporates a series of five questions to consider. They include:

1. Why is there a problem?
2. What is the problem?
3. What are possible solutions to the problem?
4. What would happen if you solved the problem in each of these ways?
5. What is the best solution to the problem?

Another useful procedure shared by Cash (2011), the I-FORD problem-solving process, uses five steps to identify a problem, gather facts, list and rank options, and then make a decision:

Identify: Define or shape the problem. What is the goal you want to achieve?

Facts: Gather the facts and data you need to make the best decision.

Options: List possible solutions or strategies to solve the problem.

Rank your options: Rate, rank, and test your options and strategies.

Decide: Make your decision and implement and evaluate your solution. (p. 163)

Once a case has been analyzed using tools like those presented above, some helpful strategies in decision making include questions (Swartz & Parks, 1994) to consider (see Figure 7 and Appendix B) along with a decision-making matrix (see Figure 8 and Appendix B).

1. What makes a decision necessary?
2. What are my options?
3. What are the likely consequences of each option?
4. How important are the consequences?
5. Which option is best in light of the consequences?

Another useful tool, the Decision Wheel (more information can be found at http://www.blueprint.edu.au/Portals/0/primary/Wisely_17_Decision_Wheel.pdf), can be used as a guide to discuss a case using the following questions (see Figure 9 and Appendix B):

1. What is the problem?
2. What are the choices you have?
3. What do you think the consequences of these choices will be for yourself and others who are involved?

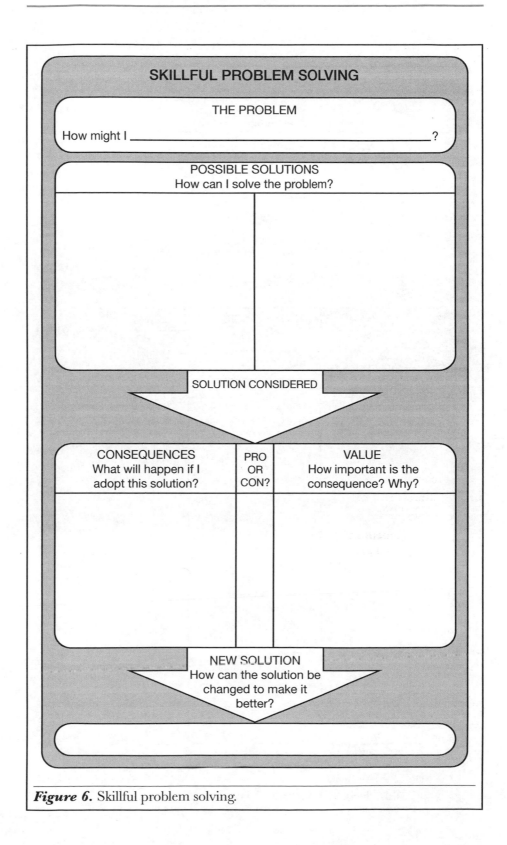

Figure 6. Skillful problem solving.

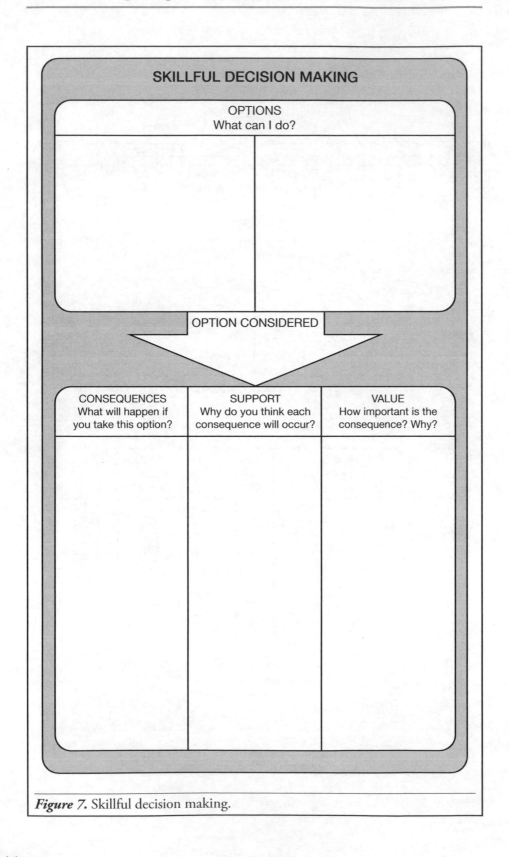

Figure 7. Skillful decision making.

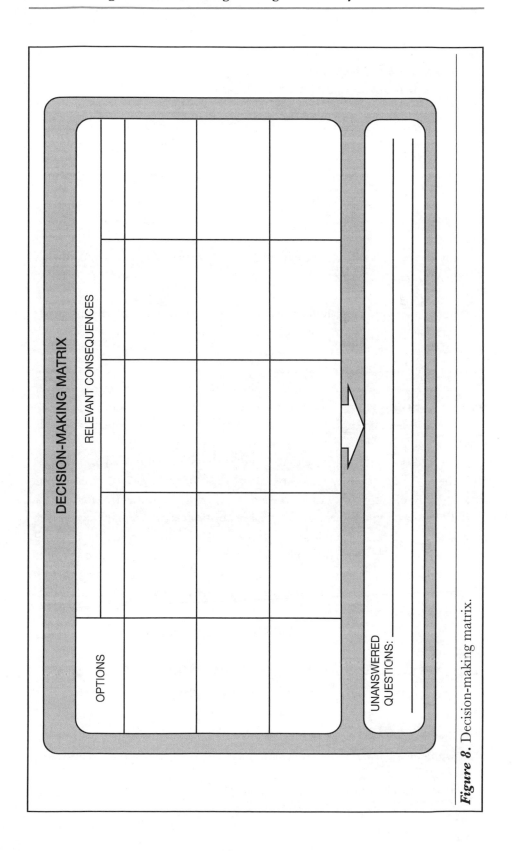

Figure 8. Decision-making matrix.

4. What values do you need to consider?
5. How do you feel about the situation?
6. Is there anything else you need to learn about it?
7. Do you need to ask for help? Who will you ask?
8. What is your decision?
9. Do you think you made the right decision? Why?

Generate possible solutions to the problem. Determine the need for criteria to weigh possible solutions such as time, costs, level of impact, etc. Evaluate the alternative solutions using the criteria selected. Draft a plan of action as necessary. Present your findings to a larger group. A conflict/resolution organizer can help identify the main conflict and events that lead to the conflict while also allowing for the consideration of events that can lead to a resolution (see Figure 10 and Appendix B).

Appendix C offers a sample case study analysis using decision-making strategies and may be helpful to review prior to the first attempt at analyzing a case. The organizers presented in this book are not exhaustive, but provide optional ways to investigate how the cases support the *NAGC Pre-K–Grade 12 Gifted Education Programming Standards* (2010) and can be used to determine a course of action in similar circumstances. They also give the reader an opportunity to become familiar with issues specific to the field of gifted education and begin to apply this understanding in new and different ways.

For additional follow-up, activities and extensions are provided for each case. It is suggested that at least one of these in both sections be used to extend thinking, thereby directing the reader toward developing an authentic product that could be utilized in another setting, personal or professional. Following this process will help the participant learn about the needs of gifted learners and hopefully improve the quality of services provided to them. It is important that any products developed be authentic in nature, meaning that they be implemented in the classroom, school, district, or other setting. The sharing of such products is also beneficial to others.

What Are Some Suggestions for Organizing Professional Development Opportunities?

The book can be used in a variety of ways to support professional or staff development for a variety of audiences. First, the book can support coursework related to preservice and in-service general education, special education, and gifted education. Other educators, such as administrators, counselors, psycholo-

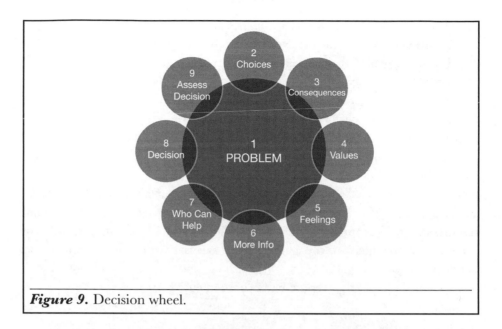

Figure 9. Decision wheel.

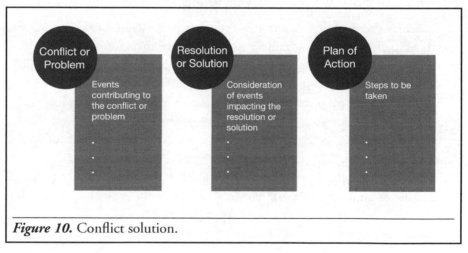

Figure 10. Conflict solution.

gists, and support staff, as well as parents can benefit from analyzing and reflecting on situations dealing with the unique needs of the gifted and talented student. Oftentimes, required texts for these classes lack real world, authentic learning scenarios that would encourage and engage the learner in critical thinking beyond the material presented in the book. This book of case studies can supplement a variety of courses while providing educators and other stakeholders the opportunities for collaborative inquiry and learning.

Second, the cases can be analyzed in a workshop format within the school setting such as Professional Learning Communities (PLC); thus, empowering staff with decision-making strategies. Astuto, Clark, Read, McGree, and Fernandez

(1993) identified *the professional community of learners* as teachers in a school and its administrators who continuously seek and share learning and then act on what they learn. The goal of their actions is to enhance their effectiveness as professionals so that students benefit. This arrangement has also been termed *communities of continuous inquiry and improvement* (Hord, 1997). The case studies provide content to enhance what Hord (1997) described as one of the results for staff, "powerful learning that defines good teaching and classroom practice and that creates new knowledge and beliefs about teaching and learners" (p. 5). In 2011, the National Staff Development Council (NSDC) published a set of standards to help guide educational leaders when creating or implementing effective professional development. The standards focus on learning communities, leadership, resources, data, learning designs, implications, and outcomes. The analysis of the cases support many of these components and is a vehicle for participants to conduct conversations about students, teaching, and learning, while identifying related issues and problems specific to educating gifted learners.

Facilitating Professional Development

You may decide that you are either going to be a facilitator of learning and lead a group discussion, or participate as an individual in a group discussion. As a facilitator of learning, whether you choose to conduct a PLC or a 1-hour, 2-hour, 3-hour, or full-day professional development workshop, or supplement reading in coursework, your preparation and familiarity with the cases will enable you to lead the discussion for your group so that all participants benefit from the discourse. The following steps will help the facilitator run an effective professional development session:

1. Determine the learning environment that is conducive to the size of the room and number of participants (e.g., need for tables, participants working in pairs, small groups, large group discussions). Decide if additional materials are needed such as a white board, chart paper, markers, etc.

2. Identify which *NAGC Pre-K–Grade 12 Gifted Education Programming Standards* (2010) are most important to address based on the needs, readiness, and interests of the group. Select the cases that support the standards identified.

3. Read each case study thoroughly so you are familiar with all aspects of the case.

4. Understand the steps for a case study analysis.

5. Select decision-making strategies that will best enhance the understanding of the case (see Appendix B).

6. Make sure each participant has a copy of this book and reads the case(s).

7. Determine which questions will be most helpful for discussion, which activities will be most appropriate for all or some of the participants, and which extensions will provide further insight and investigation for all or some of the participants. Note that as in any classroom there will be different levels of knowledge, skills, and understandings, and you may have to adjust the pace, depth, and breadth of the discussions.

8. Facilitate the case analysis by modeling critical thinking and decision-making strategies for the participants. Being a good facilitator requires listening skills and observation skills, along with knowing when and where to ask questions and elicit further discussion. Be prepared to share additional resources if needed.

9. Assign a timekeeper to ensure that adequate discussion is appropriated and an opportunity for all to participate is considered.

Depending on which activities and/or extensions are selected, the time needed to complete them will depend on the depth and complexity required for the case. Final products may take you into the next session or may actually be shared and applied within the local school, district, or other appropriate venue at a later time.

Suggested Format for a Session Agenda

Introduction—5 minutes
Reading the Case—10 minutes
Applying a Case Study Analysis—35 minutes
Reflection and Selection of Assignments and/or Extensions—10 minutes

---

Using Technology to Support Professional Development

It is important to consider how technology can support professional development especially in a field where such opportunities may be scarce, limited due to economic constraints, or even nonexistent. In learning, teaching, and professional development, technology is used with varying degrees of intensity and integration into practice. Several models of technology integration have been developed and adopted through research (Dwyer, Ringstaff, & Sandholtz, 1991; Hooper & Rieber, 1995; Moersch, 1995). The predominant levels of technology integration guide professional development and range from awareness and entry through adoption and integration to invention and transformation where the greatest potential lies for working in ways not possible without the technology. Reinventing and transforming professional development, particularly for those educators and stakeholders in gifted education might involve advances such as:

- expanding access to activities at any time;
- increasing the variety of activities, including content learning, reading and coaching, curriculum development, and advocacy;
- specializing and personalizing topics and/or activities;
- assuming greater flexibility and opportunity for self-pacing of activities; and
- recruiting a wider range of colleagues with which to interact.

Professional development activities that occur primarily in face-to-face settings can be supported by technology tools such as software, apps, and web-based resources for conducting literature reviews, reading eBooks, brainstorming, planning, managing projects, continuing discussions online between meetings, and including remote participants in meetings. These tools are easily accessible during the discussion, activities, and extensions presented in the case studies. Job-embedded online professional development programs should share a core of common practices, including community building and sustainability with ongoing facilitated support for cycles of application, learning, and reflection on outcomes. Effective online professional development programs have been developed for several purposes. For discrete knowledge and skill acquisition (Cavanaugh & Dawson, 2010), informal, individualized professional learning can update an educator's content knowledge and pedagogical content knowledge. As a formal professional learning community, a cohort-based graduate degree program can be delivered in blended or online format with a focus on identifying and addressing problems in practice (Dawson, Cavanaugh, Sessums, Black, & Kumar, 2011; Kumar, Dawson, Black, Cavanaugh, & Sessums, 2011). In support of inquiry into effective teaching practice, structured examinations of the teaching practice can be scaffolded and shared, using online systems (Dawson, Cavanaugh, & Ritzhaupt, 2012).

Reflecting on the Cases

Although it is certainly acceptable to draw a close to the case study approach after sharing responses and products between and among participants, the importance of reflection cannot be understated. Journal writing and dialogue or an interactive journal format can provide an opportunity to expand thinking and stimulate awareness of personal values and beliefs. They may be used as a vehicle for further questions or be explored or connected to other issues at a later time. Finally, reflective thinking allows for consideration of the consequences of our actions on the teaching-learning process.

Chapter 2

Recognizing Learning and Developmental Differences

Understanding the intellectual and social-emotional development of gifted and talented students is crucial to meeting their needs. These characteristics provide the basis for differentiation in curricular programs. The following cases help the reader to explore those differences and reflect on their implications.

Gifted Education Programming Standard 1: Learning and Development

This standard refers to the student learning and developmental differences found in gifted and talented learners (see Appendix A).

Claire and Response to Intervention

Introduction

Response to Intervention (RtI) is a general education initiative that addresses the learning needs of struggling learners. The process is based on a problem-solving model that uses data for decision making and is highly dependent on progress monitoring and data collection. A multidisciplinary team designs, implements, and monitors intervention plans.

This case reflects the viewpoints of Claire's teacher and principal, Claire's mother, and Claire herself.

Claire

Claire is a gifted 12-year-old. Her school offers gifted services one morning a week. She likes going to the class, but needs more. She expresses her feelings of being in the classroom as if she is trying to swim to the edge of a pool filled with mud. Claire overheard some teachers talking about a new system to help students learn, Response to Intervention (RtI). She was curious to know what they were talking about, so when she got home that afternoon, she used a search engine on the Internet to find out. She found that RtI often focuses on struggling learners. She told her mom that she thought she was struggling, too. Her mom suggested that she learn about RtI and create a persuasive argument or write a persuasive paper for her teacher or principal to review.

Claire began the process that night. During the next week, she polished her argument and asked her teacher and principal for some time after school. She informed them of her struggle against sameness, repetitive content and practice, and boredom of learning content that is too easy and that she already knows.

Mrs. Dawson, her teacher, and Dr. Hill, her principal, thanked her for her thoughtful and concise presentation. They told her they would see what they could do.

Things to Consider

- *Teachable moments are those unplanned opportunities that arise at home or in a classroom in which the ideal situation presents itself to offer insight to the learner.*
- *Struggling students are not only those who struggle to learn, but also those who struggle to learn something new. Preassessment adds insight into those students who are ready to move beyond the planned curriculum.*

Claire's School

The teacher and principal agreed that Claire had a rational idea. They further researched RtI and determined that it should include more than stereotypical struggling learners. Mrs. Dawson asked for Dr. Hill and the other sixth-grade teachers' help in designing an RtI system that meets the needs of all learners. They began by looking at the traditional RtI pyramid. They tried to think of ways to adapt it for struggling, on-level, and gifted learners. Their units of study and cluster groupings would have to be revised to meet all learners' needs. They needed to consider how much time it would take to revise lesson plans, meet state standards, and ensure positive outcomes on standardized tests.

Although Mrs. Dawson, Dr. Hill, and the other teachers realized the responsibility for curriculum development is theirs, they also enlisted the help of Claire and the other gifted sixth-grade students. They asked the students to come up with a plan for the next unit of study. The teachers believed if the students could show them how they best learn in a regular classroom and what they would produce in the study, the RtI process could be revised to include the gifted.

School district personnel looked to the NAGC Gifted Programming Standards for guidance that could facilitate the sixth graders' learning. Within *Standard 1: Learning and Development,* they explored *Student Outcomes* and *Evidence-Based Practices* (see Appendix A) in order to create the best possible learning environment for Claire and the other sixth-grade students.

Discussion Questions

1. Describe RtI. In what ways does it apply to gifted learners?
2. What best practices for the gifted could be included in a revision of units of study?
3. How can the teacher manage a classroom with students learning and producing at differing levels?
4. Is it appropriate for students to have input into curriculum? If so, when is it appropriate? If no, why not?
5. Claire described the regular classroom as a "struggle against sameness, repetitive content and practice, and boredom of learning that is too easy and content that she already knows." Is her description accurate? Why or why not? Support your point of view.
6. Should the same scale or rubric evaluate all students? If not, why? How should evaluation take place within each level of learning in the RtI pyramid?

Activities

1. Discuss one best practice, from the practices in Discussion Question #2, and explain how to use it in a primary, intermediate, and/or secondary classroom.
2. Modify an RtI pyramid to include services for gifted learners.
3. Name and describe two classroom management strategies that will facilitate RtI for all students. Share the strategies with a colleague.
4. When asking students for their input into activities within a unit of study to meet their needs, what parameters need to be established for this stu-

dent input? Create three rules to guide students in the development of activities and products.

Extensions

1. Classroom experiences for the gifted often require them to move through content at a slow pace. At times, they may feel they are "swimming in mud." What are some other analogies that describe gifted learners' experiences in a regular classroom? Make a list.
2. Research some examples of states that have implemented RtI across the board (e.g., beyond RtI for struggling learners only). Write a brief synopsis of each.
3. Dr. Susan Johnsen of Baylor University and Dr. Mary Ruth Coleman of University of North Carolina, Chapel Hill addressed RtI for gifted and talented students through a webinar with the National Association for Gifted Children and a variety of publications, including the *NAGC Pre-K–Grade 12 Gifted Education Programming Standards* (2010). Presentations through the CEC-TAG are also available through that organization. Research the national point of view toward RtI and present a synthesis of your findings.
4. Develop a timeline for revision on a unit of study to meet the needs of the gifted.
5. Revise a unit of study to meet the needs of the gifted in the regular classroom.

Additional Readings

Boswell, C., & Carlile, V. (2010). *RtI for the gifted*. Hawthorne, NJ: Educational Impressions.

Carlile, V. (2009). *Enigmas*. Hawthorne, NJ: Educational Impressions.

Carlile, V., & Burnett, T. (2009). *Creative experiences in U.S. history*. Hawthorne, NJ: Educational Impressions.

Coil, C. (2004). *Standards-based activities and assessments for the differentiated classroom*. Marion, IL: Pieces of Learning.

Coleman, J. S., Campbell, E. Q., Hobson, C. J., McPartland, J., Mood, A. M., Weinfeld, F. D., & York, R. L. (1966). *Equality of educational opportunity* (OE-38001). Washington, DC: U.S. Government Printing Office. Retrieved from http://library.sc.edu/digital/collections/eeoci.pdf

Colman, M. R., & Johnsen. S. K. (Eds.). (2011). *RtI for gifted students*. Waco, TX: Prufrock Press.

Davidson, K., & Decker, T. (2006). *Bloom's and beyond: Higher level questions and activities for the creative classroom.* Marion, IL: Pieces of Learning.

Davis, G. (n.d.). *CPS* (notes from *Creativity is forever*). Dubuque, IA: Kendall Hunt. Retrieved from http://members.optusnet.com.au/~charles57/Creative/Brain/cps.htm

EdHelper.com. (n.d.). *Critical thinking* [Online subscription service]. Retrieved from http://www.edhelper.com/critical_thinking.htm

Indiana Department of Education, Office of High Ability Education. (2011). *Tiered curriculum project.* Retrieved from http://www.doe.in.gov/achievement/individualized-learning/tiered-curriculum-project

Marzano, R. J., Pickering, D. J., & Pollock, J. E. (2001). *Classroom instruction that works: Research-based strategies for increasing student achievement.* Alexandria, VA: ASCD.

Regina Public Schools and Saskatchewan Learning. (2003). *Best practices: Instructional strategies and techniques.* Retrieved from http://www.saskschools.ca/curr_content/bestpractice/tiered/index.html

Reis, S. M., Burns, D. E., & Renzulli, J. E. (1992). *Curriculum compacting: The complete guide to modifying the regular curriculum for high ability students.* Waco, TX: Prufrock Press.

Tomlinson, C. A. (1999). *The differentiated classroom: Responding to the needs of all learners.* Alexandria, VA: ASCD.

Whitten, E., Esteves, K., & Woodrow, A. (2008). *RtI success: Proven tools and strategies for schools and classrooms.* Minneapolis, MN: Free Spirit Publishing.

Wright, J. (2007). *RtI toolkit: A practical guide for schools.* Port Chester, NY: Dude Publishing.

Wyatt

Introduction

The school or home environment may influence underachievement in some content areas and its intensity in both in-school and out-of-school spheres. Knowing when to both push and pull creates dilemmas for educators, parents, and students alike.

Wyatt's case study introduces the professional to a 13-year-old seventh-grade student who exhibits diverse learning strengths and interests influenced by his age and school environment.

The case is told from the point of view of Wyatt's school, Wyatt's parents, and Wyatt himself.

Wyatt comes from a middle-class family living in a small city in the south. His father owns his own business that he started 15 years before. The community knows his mother as the top CPA. Both contribute time and energy to their children and to community activities. Wyatt has a sister, Selena, who is 4 years older than he is. Selena focuses her school efforts on debate and theater. She and Wyatt share many common interests despite their age differences and differing abilities.

The School's Point of View

Wyatt is the star receiver on the seventh-grade football team and the high-scoring player on the basketball team. He also runs the high hurdles better than anyone in his school, including the eighth graders. Until this year, he was among the top of his class. In elementary school, he always made the highest grades within his class. He also won every science and history fair that he entered. This year, the only classes that seem to motivate him are English and science.

The methods used to identify Wyatt in the third grade were his IQ test score of 140 and his completion of a portfolio that included writing and poetry examples, which were one of his areas of interest at that time. Wyatt also indicated he was interested in solar power and won first place in the science fair with a solar powered iPod. His portfolio narrative explained that while it had been an interest of his, he had really learned all he wanted about solar power and currently was more interested in writing. Evaluations of the portfolio indicated that Wyatt was at least 2 years ahead of his classmates in creative writing, poetry, and vocabulary.

Wyatt has excelled in all academic areas until this year, even though his composite achievement scores remain high with each core content area in the

95th–99th percentile range. His teachers acknowledge that Wyatt is gifted, but are concerned that he has chosen to concentrate his efforts in only athletics and two subjects, English and science.

Parents' Point of View

Wyatt's parents are not especially concerned about his disinterest in math and social studies this school year because they know that he is going through puberty. They also notice that he enjoys the validation he receives for his efforts in athletics. With his focus on athletics, he seems to concentrate only on the academic areas related to his personal interests. They note that he has found a new interest, music, and that it takes up much of his time outside of school.

They know that Wyatt can be as successful in all of his academics as he is with athletics and his current areas of interest. They know he can excel in all areas and want him to do so, as this will allow him to pursue his interests in the college of his choice.

Wyatt's parents are meeting with his counselor and principal to discuss Wyatt's academics. They want to see what is available for him to take next school year; what is available for summer enrichment; and what he needs to graduate with a high school diploma that goes beyond minimum requirements. His parents have asked that Wyatt join them for this meeting.

Things to Consider

- *Parents' perspectives are often different from those of educators' because they see the student in a different environment.*
- *Middle school environments are very different from that of an elementary school.*
- *Underachievement occurs when a child's performance is below what is expected based on the child's ability.*

Wyatt's Point of View

Wyatt likes school the way it is at his middle school. He notes that middle school is very different from elementary school. He realizes that although he has more freedom to explore his interests, he has responsibilities to his school, to teachers, and to other students. He notices that his friendships are changing according to interests and abilities in both athletics and academics. He also notices that along with the physical changes in his own body and those of his friends, emotional changes are also occurring that create changes among social groups. Although interests dictate most of his social group, his physical ability related to changes in his body and his emotional point of view influences which students are also his associates. Even though he has preferences for friends, he is included in all social functions in and out of school.

Wyatt likes the way his science and English teachers treat him. He works hard in their classes because he likes the rigor of the classroom. His science teacher was a biologist for a pharmaceutical company before deciding to teach. She recognizes that Wyatt and two other students are more advanced than the others, so she offers them problems to solve based on her work within the pharmacy industry. Wyatt often gets so involved in the problem solving that he and his friends stay through lunch to work on the problem. They enjoy the challenge and the rigorous work they do. Wyatt always thinks about the problem before him or the implications of the outcome. Wyatt also spends time on the Internet exploring sites that relate to projects offered by his science teacher. He is very interested in chemical reactions in general, and how they influence the combination of prescribed medicine with over the counter medications. His teacher has sparked a fascination with chemical reactions that has opened the world of chemistry to him. The teacher believes that he should be able to move into high school chemistry next year.

His English teacher has recognized his ability to write, especially poetry. When Mr. Menzel knows that Wyatt has mastered what the class is studying, he gives him references about poets and asks him to emulate them with an original poem of his own. Wyatt has learned a great deal about poetry this year through this approach. He believes he can develop his own style once he learns about other successful poets.

At home, Wyatt listens to and writes music. He even wrote a piece of music and lyrics for a song in one of his sister's theater productions. He has learned that he can set many of his poems to music, and spends much of his leisure time with his guitar and poetry.

He does not have to work hard in math and social studies. The teachers are boring to him and the work is not challenging. Wyatt takes mind trips during math class, as it seems to him that the teacher does not know as much as he already does. He does his homework, but sees no point in contributing in the class and continues doing the minimal amount of work possible. All of the repetition is boring to him. His science teacher tells him that he needs to know math to work with all areas of science, including chemistry.

Social studies used to be his favorite subject because his teachers would tell stories to go along with the history, and talk about why an era was important. This year, it is only facts, dates, and locations on the map. Wyatt can memorize them, but he really wants the backstory, the history to the history. He is tired of memorizing for the sake of memorizing.

Wyatt is good at athletics, and everyone in his middle school likes him because of his abilities. He compares athletics and academics by relating that all of his physical activity within athletics feels as good to his body as writing poetry or solving problems feels to his mind.

The Challenge

School district personnel look to the NAGC Programming Standards for guidance in meeting the needs of Wyatt's parents and Wyatt. Each perspective presents its own challenge. The school must explore a variety of possibilities and solutions to meet learners' needs, The guidance offered by *Standard 1: Learning and Development, Student Outcomes and Evidence-Based Practices*, facilitates the creation of the best possible learning environment for Wyatt.

Discussion Questions

1. What special needs does Wyatt have? What course of action would you recommend for his eighth-grade year? Why?
2. What specific questions should Wyatt's parents ask the counselor? Are there other questions they should ask the principal? Why?
3. If Wyatt's parents disagree with the school, what is their course of action?
4. If the school disagrees with the desires of Wyatt's parents, what is their course of action?
5. Is Wyatt gifted? In what ways? What would you tell Wyatt's parents about his abilities/gifts?
6. What would you tell Wyatt about his abilities/gifts? How do you believe Wyatt would respond to a question that asks what it means to be considered gifted before any explanation? How do you believe he would respond after an explanation?

Activities

1. Conduct research on Dabrowski's overexcitabilities. Do any of the areas of overexcitability apply to Wyatt? If so, which one(s) and how? Describe the area(s) that apply to Wyatt and how his overexcitability can be used to his best advantage. Modify a unit of study you would use to accommodate Wyatt's area of overexcitability, in order to facilitate his academic growth.
2. Create an outline of a semester of brown-bag lunch sessions for gifted middle school students that explore the concept of *giftedness*.
3. Research some out-of-school options available for middle school gifted students in your area.

Extensions

1. Brown bag lunches can provide an opportunity to explore social and emotional needs of gifted students. Develop a brown-bag lunch session with an outline and two activities for gifted middle school students.
2. Determine an issue relevant to your gifted child or one in your school district. Select participants and conduct a role-play to include the parent(s), a counselor, the principal, and/or the G/T coordinator.

Additional Readings

Colangelo, N., Kerr, B., Christensen, P., & Maxey, J. (2004). A comparison of gifted underachievers and gifted high achievers. In S. M. Reis (Series Ed.) & S. M. Moon (Vol. Ed.), *Essential readings in gifted education series: Vol. 8. Social/emotional issues, underachievement, and counseling of gifted and talented students* (pp. 119–132). Thousand Oaks, CA: Corwin Press.

Davidson, J., & Davidson, B. (with Vanderkam, L.). (2004). *Genius denied: How to stop wasting our brightest young minds.* New York, NY: Simon and Schuster. Retrieved from http://www.geniusdenied.com

Delisle, J., & Galbraith, J. (2002). *When gifted kids don't have all the answers: How to meet their social and emotional needs.* Minneapolis, MN: Free Spirit.

Galbraith, J., & Delisle, J. (2011). *The gifted teen survival guide: Smart, sharp, and ready for (almost) anything* (4th ed.). Minneapolis, MN: Free Spirit.

Hoover-Schultz, B. (2005). Gifted underachievement: Oxymoron or educational enigma? In S. K. Johnsen & J. Kendrick (Eds.), *Teaching strategies in gifted education* (pp. 127–136). Waco, TX: Prufrock Press. Retrieved from http://www.mcrgroup.org/bogota/Resources/Articles/Schultz.pdf

Kaplan, S., & Cannon, M. W. (2001). *Lessons from the middle: High-end learning for middle school students.* Waco, TX: Prufrock Press.

National Association for Gifted Children. (2008). *Meeting the needs of high ability and high potential learners in the middle grades* [Position statement]. Retrieved from http://www.nagc.org/index.aspx?id=400

Rakow, S. (2011). *Educating gifted students in middle school: A practical guide* (2nd ed.). Waco, TX: Prufrock Press.

Tillier, B. (1995, October 26). *The theory of positive disintegration by Kazimierz Dabrowski* [Synopsis bibliography]. Retrieved from http://positivedisintegration.com/#synopsisbibliography

Tomlinson, C. A. (1995). *Gifted learners and the middle school: Problem or promise?* [ERIC EC Digest E535]. Retrieved from http://www.nagc.org/index.aspx?id=150

U.S. Department of Education, Office of Educational Research and Improvement. (1993). *National excellence: A case for developing America's talent.* Washington,

DC: Author. Retrieved from https://www.ocps.net/cs/ese/programs/gifted/Documents/National%20Excellence_%20A%20Case%20for%20Developing%20America's%20Talent_%20Introduction.pdf

Walker, S. Y. (2002). *The survival guide for parents of gifted kids: How to understand, live with, and stick up for your gifted child* (Rev. ed.). Minneapolis, MN: Free Spirit.

Jessica

Introduction

It is often difficult to identify gifted and talented learners with learning disabilities. These unique learners have remarkable strengths in one or more areas and significant weaknesses in others. According to Susan Baum (2004), these students can be grouped into three categories: students identified as gifted who also have subtle learning disabilities; students identified as having a learning disability, but not identified as gifted; and unidentified students whose giftedness and learning disabilities mask each other so that the student functions at or slightly below grade level.

Jessica's case study introduces the professional to an 11-year-old student and past participant in the elementary gifted program. Jessica's parents are concerned about the apparent discrepancy between their daughter's efforts and achievement.

Jessica comes from an intact middle-class family, living in a small Midwestern community. Her father owns his own business, and her mother is an elementary school teacher. The family values education and begins dinner each evening by asking the children about their school day. If time allows, the conversation typically turns to current events.

At 11, Jessica is arguably one of the most well-liked girls in the sixth grade. Friends describe her as smart, cute, and fun. They envy her ability to get along with everyone—popular kids, smart kids, "jocks", and "nerds" all like Jessica. She swims competitively, has a great voice, and knows the lyrics to "all" the songs. Last year, when Jessica was cast as the lead in a summer stock production of *Annie,* family and friends filled the audience.

Although classroom work is not easy for Jessica, she loves attending school. She likes interacting with her classmates and enjoys several of her classes. She finds science interesting, especially class demonstrations and experiments. She actively participates in social studies and language arts class discussions, but finds keeping up with the reading to be an ongoing challenge. Choir is her favorite, and math is a struggle.

Things to Consider

- *Expectations for middle school students are not the same as those for elementary students. Sixth graders typically experience increased homework and reading assignments upon entering middle school.*
- *Study skills and time management are learned behaviors.*

Teachers enjoy Jessica in class, describing her as a "respectful and conscientious student." Comments shared during conferences and on report cards indicate her assignments are thorough and on time. Although group work, experiential learning, and projects are particular strengths for Jessica, classroom and achievement test scores are typically in the average to low-average range. This is somewhat surprising given her third-grade Cognitive Abilities Test (CogAT) score of 129 and past participation in the elementary gifted program.

Although Jessica's mother is worried about her daughter, colleagues at school have confirmed with assurance that Jessica is a "great kid, doing just fine." When Jessica admits during her sixth-grade conference that homework at times can seem overwhelming, her teachers are surprised. They assume her contributions to class discussions reflect a wide range of knowledge and above-average reading ability. They are not aware that Jessica reads very slowly, often rereading passages many times for basic comprehension. They have no idea how hard she works or how frustrated she is about schoolwork.

With an eye on the future, Jessica's parents are concerned her test scores and grades are not an accurate indication of their daughter's ability. They worry about state assessments required for graduation and college entrance exams. Jessica realizes she spends far more time on her homework than her peers and is beginning to wonder if something is wrong. Jessica questions her own capability, and whether school administration will permit her to take the enriched and accelerated courses that interest her.

Discussion Questions

1. Based on the *NAGC Pre-K–Grade 12 Gifted Education Programming Standard 1: Learning and Development Student Outcomes 1.1 Self-Understanding* (see Appendix A) referencing self-understanding, is Jessica a gifted student? If so, in what areas does she exhibit gifted characteristics? Does she demonstrate self-knowledge with respect to her interests, strengths, identity, and needs in social-emotional development and in

intellectual, academic, creative, leadership, or artistic domains? What evidence supports your choice(s)? What seem to be Jessica's special needs? What possible course of action might one take to address those needs?

2. What type of assessment is likely to provide the most accurate picture of Jessica's strengths and relative weaknesses? Why? Who should assess Jessica?
3. What conversation, if any, would you have with Jessica prior to assessment?
4. Why were Jessica's needs and her parent's concerns overlooked?

Activities

1. Develop a plan to present Jessica's case to the school Child Study Team. Determine who should comprise the team and what information is pertinent to the case.
2. Create a decision-making tree for the assessment and intervention decisions for students suspected of twice-exceptionality.
3. Conduct research on reading problems. Does Jessica exhibit characteristics consistent with reading problems? If so, what intervention or support can provide her with the help she needs? Share your findings with a colleague.
4. Research the Javits Grant 2XCEL (http://www.stthomas.edu/project2excel/), identify support and resource materials for twice-exceptional learners. List your top five materials.

Extensions

1. Plan and record a webinar that raises awareness of twice-exceptional learners.
2. Create an annotated bibliography of current research in literacy that focuses on gifted learners with reading problems.
3. Research one other type of learning disability that influences the perceptions of giftedness. Present your findings using a product of your choice.

Additional Readings

Besnoy, K. D. (2006). *Successful strategies for twice-exceptional students.* Waco, TX: Prufrock Press.

Heacox, D. (2009). *Making differentiation a habit: How to ensure success in academically diverse classrooms.* Minneapolis, MN: Free Spirit Publishing.

Johnsen, S. K. (2005). *Identifying gifted students: A step-by-step guide.* Waco, TX: Prufrock Press.

Rakow, S. (2011). *Educating gifted students in middle school: A practical guide* (2nd ed.). Waco, TX: Prufrock Press.

Rogers, K. B. (2002). *Re-forming gifted education: Matching the program to the child.* Scottsdale, AZ: Great Potential Press.

Salembier, G. B. (1999). Scan and run: A reading comprehension strategy that works. *Journal of Adolescent and Adult Literacy, 42,* 386–394.

Walpole, S., & McKenna, M. C. (2007). *Differentiated reading instruction: Strategies for the primary grades.* New York, NY: Guilford Press.

Winebrenner, S. (2003). Teaching strategies for twice-exceptional students. *Intervention in School and Clinic, 38,*131–137.

Chapter 3

Assessing Learning Progress and Evaluating Services

Identification of students for services is a critical component of providing students with a challenging and appropriate education. Best practices in the identification of gifted and talented learners require the consideration of multiple measures of student achievement and potential. Assessments and procedures should be valid as well as reliable, fair, and based on current research and theory. Checklists, inventories, portfolios, observations, and nominations also provide valuable information.

Assessment information relates to the identification process of gifted and talented students, the evaluation of a student's learning, and the evaluation of program effectiveness. It is important to remember that the evaluation of an individual's learning contributes to the evaluation of the effectiveness of a program. The following case outlines the complex issues related to assessment of students for services.

Gifted Education Programming Standard 2: Assessment

This standard focuses on all aspects of assessment including assessment for identification, assessment of learning progress, and evaluation of program services, thus providing information about student learning and developmental differences found in gifted and talented learners (see Appendix A).

Eric, Assessment, and Services

Introduction

Pre- and postassessments are essential to determine learning progress. Services provided to gifted and talented learners sometimes reflect these assessments' use, misuse, and/or lack of use. Eric's case reveals a middle school student with little emotional and monetary support. Although highly gifted, he is very close to being unable to pass the seventh grade. The school has not made accommodations for his intellectual or emotional needs. This case illustrates the problems an administrator faces to ensure appropriate pre- and postassessment of learning and its impact on highly gifted children. Highlighted through Eric's case is the need to evaluate the relationship of teaching and learning outcomes for the gifted and talented.

Eric

Eric is a 13-year-old, seventh-grade student in a middle school housing grades 6, 7, and 8. He lives with his mother, who is often absent from the home. When she is gone, Eric stays with a friend, whose mother makes sure Eric is clean and fed. Eric seems to realize he is in charge of himself and takes much of the responsibility for his learning, or lack of it.

Eric is coded in district documents as Hispanic, low socioeconomic (SES), and at-risk. The household includes Eric and his mother. His mother works sporadically at minimum wage jobs. To help with bills, Eric mows lawns and does other odd jobs in his neighborhood and for his friends' parents. Eric does not have access to the Internet at home, but has a library card and spends much of his spare time at the public library surfing the Internet and finding books to take home to read. Eric has recently become an aide at the school library; he says it is his nirvana or paradise.

Eric's Campus

The campus is one of six middle schools in a district of 15,000 students. Eric's campus houses 475 students. This campus, built in 2000, serves as a neighborhood middle school, but also buses in students from another section of town in order to meet the capacity of the building. The table on page 51 includes statistics for this campus and the district as a whole.

Category	Percentage of Campus	Percentage of District
Hispanic	73	55
African American	25	31
White	2	11
Economically Disadvantaged	96	87
Gifted and Talented (G/T)	11	8
Limited English Proficient (LEP)	21	17
Special Education	15	11
At Risk	69	68
Students With Disciplinary Placements	10	6
Mobility	25	22

As you can see, this campus is in a neighborhood with the majority of its population consisting of among Hispanic and more economically disadvantaged students than the district as a whole. Even though there are more Limited English Proficient (LEP), special education students, students with disciplinary placements, and a slightly higher mobility rate, there are more identified gifted students than the district average. Although these statistics bear a closer look, this case focuses on the learning needs of Eric and other gifted students like him on this campus.

Eric's Conundrum

Eric's science teacher brought Eric to the attention of the director for gifted services because she believed that he should be taking Pre-Advanced Placement (Pre-AP) science instead of the regular seventh-grade science class. The teacher indicated that although his grades were not good, he asked probing questions. When the director and campus counselor looked at Eric's grades, they found that he was failing everything but English. A deeper look showed that Eric had not turned in daily work, resulting in many zeros. Conversely, all of his unit tests' grades were in the 90s with several 100s. When the district G/T director asked if the teachers preassessed Eric for prior knowledge, all teachers said that they did not preassess.

The counselor and the district G/T director also looked up data used to identify Eric as gifted. Even though he had moved often during his years of school, data were available from all schools (see Figure 11), not only his identification data for gifted services, but also his report card grades.

	Below Average	Average	Strong Average	Excellent	Superior
District Line: Minimum of 2					
School Ability (IQ)	<85	85–99	100–115	116–129	130+
• OLSAT or SAGES-2 Reasoning (K–8) or CogAT or NNAT or other School Ability test as appropriate					**166**
Achievement Scores (percentiles)	≤50	51–80	81–90	91–95	96–99
• SAGES-2 Math/Science (K–8) or ITBS or MAT8 or other achievement test as appropriate			**90**		
• SAGES-2 ELA/SS (K–8) of ITBS or MAT8 or other achievement test as appropriate					**99**
Divergent Thinking	≤85	85–100	101–116	116–131	131+
• Torrance Test of Creative Thinking				**127**	
Elementary Teacher Rating Scales (GATES, Standard Scores)					
• Intellectual Ability	<70	70–79	80–89	90–109	**111+**
• Academic Skills	<70	70–79	80–89	90–109	**111+**
• Creativity	<70	70–79	80–89	90–109	**111+**
• Leadership	<70	70–79	**80–89**	90–109	111+
• Artistic Talent	<70	70–79	**80–89**	90–109	111+
Parent Rating Scale (GATES, Standard Scores)					
• Intellectual Ability	<70	70–79	**80–89**	90–109	111+
• Academic Skills	<70	70–79	**80–89**	90–109	111+
• Creativity	<70	70–79	**80–89**	90–109	111+
• Leadership	<70	70–79	**80–89**	90–109	111+
• Artistic Talent	<70	70–79	**80–89**	90–109	111+
Student Interview or Other Qualitative Data	1	2	3	4	5
• Product				**X**	

Figure 11. Little ISD gifted/talented identification profile for student #60123 (Eric's scores are in bold). *Note:* OLSAT= Otis Lennon School Ability Test®; SAGES-2= Screening Assessment for Gifted Elementary Students; CogAT= Cognitive Abilities Test; NNAT= Naglieri Nonverbal Ability Test®; ITBS= Iowa Test of Basic Skills; MAT8= Metropolitan Achievement Test [8th ed.]; GATES= Gifted and Talented Evaluation Scales

	English	Math	Social Studies	Science
Grade 1	100	100	100	100
Grade 2	98	97	97	98
Grade 3	99	99	99	97
Grade 4	98	95	96	96
Grade 5	95	90	94	92
Grade 6	90	70	88	86
Grade 7 (first semester)	80	50	60	60

Figure 12. Eric's report cards—final grades.

The administrators expressed that district policy does not require reassessment, and they noted that this had not occurred for Eric since Grade 1. At this point, it seemed appropriate for them to take a closer look at Eric's grades throughout his school years, which can be seen in Figure 12.

It was obvious to school personnel, based on Eric's final grades in his early school years, that both his learning and grades matched his intellectual ability. The downhill slide began in grade 5 and accelerated to its current level. The counselor and director decided it was in Eric's best interest to meet with all interested parties, including Eric and his mother.

The Meeting

The district G/T director contacted the counselor to set up a meeting for all parties: Eric and his mother; his science, math, English, and social studies teachers; and the counselor. The meeting opened a can of worms. Once Eric learned the purpose of the meeting, the floodgates of his thoughts opened. Eric talked about his lack of interest in school, and he adamantly stated that he only likes to read (his current reading level was 12.1). He expressed that in science they only watch films, take notes, and answer questions, and noted that he could learn all of this by simply reading. He talked about history class in much the same way. He said he liked English, but hated to write. He stated, "I have it all in my head and it takes too much time to write it all down. Can't I just tell someone what I am thinking?" When questioned about his low grades in math, Eric responded, "I just don't get math. The teacher goes too fast and I just don't understand it." This statement brought perplexed looks from all of those present. The group pondered on how a student with such a high IQ and good math grades until grade 5, could make such a statement. The math situation seemed different from his problems in other classes. His mother offered little to the discussion, except to say that he was very good in math until the third or fourth grade. She said he began to lose interest in it and spent all of his time reading. The school personnel decided to focus on the grades he could easily bring up and address his math problems in other ways.

Things to Consider

- *What is the relationship of grades to learning?*
- *What is the role of preassessment?*
- *How can academic growth be measured?*

The discussion centered on Eric's needs to be successful. How could the teachers and administrators create an environment for learning that valued Eric's current knowledge and measured his academic growth?

Eric agreed to make an effort toward raising his grades if the teachers would make learning more relevant for him. The teachers and administrators recognized that not all teaching leads to learning, especially in the case of learners like Eric. Eric's problems were not unique to middle school. The G/T director found that very few teachers across the district used any form of preassessment. Postassessment was limited to unit or chapter tests, and very few teachers used performance or products in lieu of paper-and-pencil tests. School personnel looked to the *NAGC Pre-K–Grade 12 Gifted Education Programming Standards* (2010) for guidance.

A Plan for Eric

With this data, input from Eric, suggestions from campus personnel, and the Programming Standards, it was determined that he would move into all Pre-AP classes except math. Preassessment would be offered to Eric in all of his Pre-AP classes, and he would begin independent study in classes in which he demonstrated prior knowledge and mastery of the subject. His work, whether regular daily work or with the independent study, would constitute daily grades so that he had something to turn in every time all other students turned in daily work. Eric was told that if he kept up his part with daily work, the teachers would keep up their part with preassessment.

Discussion Questions

1. Was Eric's identification profile appropriate? Discuss what the profile shows about Eric as a learner.
2. In what ways does Eric's identification profile mirror his current learning needs?
3. How might the school evaluate Eric's learning (see Appendix A; *Standard 2 Assessment Student Outcomes 2.5 Evaluation of Programming*)?
4. Is the plan for Eric a viable one? Why or why not?
5. In what ways can one accommodate Eric's current reading level of 12.1? How can one accommodate his 166 IQ?
6. In what ways does Eric's situation reflect on the relationship of teaching and learning?

Activities

1. Develop a pre-and postassessment for a student you know, applying *Standard 2: Assessment Evidence-Based Practices 2.4.1* and *2.4.2* (see Appendix A).
2. Describe at least two off-level standardized assessments to measure the progress of the student in Activity #1. Give reasons for your selections.
3. Develop a profile of Eric's strengths and weaknesses based on his identification profile and grades from Grades 1–4 and from Grades 5–7.
4. Create a research-based unit of study for Eric that would meet his needs in seventh-grade math. Include not only skills, but also pre-and post-assessments. Using at least three resources, include activities that meet his learning needs and strengths.
5. Develop an outline for an independent study unit for an advanced or gifted student that addresses a high reading level, a middle school-aged student, and learning strengths in the humanities.

Extensions

1. Research growth models related to gifted and advanced learners. Create a chart that compares the models. Determine the most appropriate model for your campus or district.
2. Develop a classroom management plan to accommodate all learners in a mixed-ability classroom. Include a floor plan of the classroom.
3. In what ways could a campus or district change the curriculum for highly gifted and advanced learners? Give at least three specific changes.
4. Conduct research on district evaluation plans. Select or create one that would meet the needs of your campus or district.

Additional Readings

Coil, C. (2004). *Standards-based activities and assessment for the differentiated classroom.* Marion, IL: Pieces of Learning.

Colangelo, N., Assouline, S. G., & Gross, M. U. M. (2004). *A nation deceived: How schools hold back America's brightest students* (Vol. 1) Iowa City: University of Iowa, The Connie Belin & Jacqueline N. Blank International Center for Gifted Education and Talent Development. Retrieved from http://www.education.uiowa.edu/belinblank/pdfs/ND_v1.pdf

Colangelo, N., Kerr, B., Christensen, P., & Maxey, J. (2004). A comparison of gifted underachievers and gifted high achievers. In S. M. Reis (Series Ed.) & S. M. Moon (Vol. Ed.), *Essential readings in gifted education series: Vol. 8. Social/emotional issues, underachievement, and counseling of gifted and talented students* (pp. 119–132). Thousand Oaks, CA: Corwin Press.

Davidson, J., & Davidson, B. (with Vanderkam, L.). (2004). *Genius denied: How to stop wasting our brightest young minds.* New York, NY: Simon and Schuster. Retrieved from http://www.geniusdenied.com

Delisle, J., & Galbraith, J. (2002). *When gifted kids don't have all the answers: How to meet their social and emotional needs.* Minneapolis, MN: Free Spirit.

Hoover-Schultz, B. (2005). Removing the mask: How to identify and develop giftedness in students from poverty? In S. K. Johnsen & J. Kendrick (Eds.), *Teaching strategies in gifted education* (pp. 127–136). Waco, TX: Prufrock Press. Retrieved from http://www.mcrgroup.org/bogota/Resources/Articles/Schultz.pdf

Tomlinson, C. A. (1995). *Gifted learners and the middle school: Problem or promise?* [ERIC EC Digest E535]. Retrieved from http://www.nagc.org/index.aspx?id=150

Tomlinson, C. A. (1999). *The differentiated classroom: Responding to the needs of all learners.* Alexandria, VA: ASCD.

U.S. Department of Education, Office of Educational Research and Improvement. (1993). *National excellence: A case for developing America's talent.* Washington, DC: Author. Retrieved from https://www.ocps.net/cs/ese/programs/gifted/Documents/National%20Excellence_%20A%20Case%20for%20Developing%20America's%20Talent_%20Introduction.pdf

Dumont Public School District

Introduction

The focus of this case study is to provide the education professional with an overview of the complexity of the identification of gifted learners in a highly diverse school district. Dumont Public School District's case study introduces educators to some of the challenges of creating an identification system that is nonbiased and equitable. This case illustrates the need to create local norms, alternative paths for identification, and professional development to inform staff of the unique needs of traditionally underrepresented populations.

Dumont Public School District (DPSD) is an urban district with a K–12 enrollment of just under 40,000 students. The district is located in Dumont, a historic port city, founded in close proximity to early Native American settlements as a trading and transportation center. Today, the vibrant city is highly diverse, densely populated, and a center for government, business, and cultural activities.

Families who enroll their children in DPSD may select from 65 sites and numerous school configurations to find the best fit for their children. Although neighborhood schools are popular, families may also choose among traditional schools, grade level centers, charter schools, magnet schools, or special education sites. Early childhood education serving children from birth to age 5 is available at 12 additional sites. International Baccalaureate (IB) programs are available at three high schools, and the Primary Years IB program at four elementary schools.

As with many urban centers throughout the United States, Dumont's dynamic population has experienced an influx of immigrants and refugees. During the past 10 years, the district's English language learner (ELL) population grew 240%; by comparison, the entire district enrollment increased 7%. Dumont's ELL population currently represents 41% of the district population and 25% of the state ELL population.

Students attending schools in (DPSD) speak more than 80 languages and dialects. The most common languages spoken are: English 21,775; Hmong 9,658; Spanish 4,194; Somali 885; Burmese/Karen 627; Vietnamese 346; Oromo 265; and Amharic 231. Many of the students are new immigrants and more than 40% are refugees. More than 45% of the students live in homes in which English is not the first language spoken.

Both the district and state anticipate continued growth in the ELL population as new refugees continue to arrive and are most likely to settle where they have family or within a thriving immigrant community. Resettlement agencies predict future immigrants will include Somalis, Burmese, Vietnamese, and Nepalese.

Things to Consider

When developing identification procedures that ensure equal access educators must ask (Johnsen, 2005):

- *What steps will be included in the identification procedure?*
- *What assessments will be used during each step?*
- *Who will serve on the selection committee? How will they be trained?*
- *What due process procedures will be initiated?*
- *How will equal access be ensured throughout all steps? (p. 32)*

Last year, more than 75% of Dumont's students qualified for free and reduced lunch under the federally subsidized program ensuring all students are fed, regardless of their ability to pay. A reported 2,000 students are homeless, although there is growing concern the number is underreported.

With growing poverty and the rapidly increasing enrollment of the ELL student, it has become apparent that the district's identification protocol needs changes. The population identified for gifted services no longer mirrors the district population, and district staff and community activists have leveled charges of discrimination.

For the past 5 years, the district has given all elementary students enrolled in grades K–5 a nonverbal ability test to establish the pool of students considered for gifted services. Under the current system, students who score in the 93rd percentile or above on the nonverbal test qualify for gifted services. For students receiving a score in the 87th–92nd percentile, a portfolio is created and reviewed. When complete, the portfolio includes several performance tasks, parent and teacher checklists, achievement data, and an assessment of mathematical reasoning. Despite best efforts, the identified gifted and talented population remains disproportionately White and Asian.

Discussion Questions

1. What issues related to meeting the needs of gifted learners do the data presented in this case imply?
2. In what ways might DPSD reduce disproportionality in its gifted programs?
3. *Standard 2: Assessment of Student Outcomes 2.2 Identification* (see Appendix A) focuses on using and interpreting a variety of assessment

evidence. What are some of the barriers to identifying gifted learners from ELL, disadvantaged, and underrepresented populations? What methodology can we use to identify students in an equitable, efficient, and nonbiased way? What special skills and training do educators need to prepare them to recognize and respond to the needs of promising learners from disadvantaged and underrepresented populations? When and how should educators acquire these skills?

4. What, if any, roles or responsibilities do community members have in the identification of students for gifted education services? What are some ways in which their input and support can be solicited?

5. What are the benefits of using performance tasks in the identification of gifted learners? How might performance tasks be integrated into Dumont's system of identification? What, if any, special provisions should the district make to ensure the tasks are nonbiased and culturally fair?

6. In local control states, do services drive the identification of students or does the identification protocol drive the services that the school provides? Which should be designed first, the identification protocol or student services? Why?

Activities

1. Research and summarize the benefits of three identification instruments, including one standardized assessment, one nontraditional assessment, and one inventory or checklist. Create a visual aid to use in a presentation to the school board and/or at a cabinet-level meeting.

2. Identify the critical issues and steps for teachers to create portfolios representative of students from diverse backgrounds to use in the identification of students for services. Determine what data should be included in the portfolio for two of the following students:
   - a student who is learning disabled,
   - a student who is an English language learner,
   - a student who is creative,
   - a student who is visually impaired,
   - a student who exhibits leadership skills,
   - a student who is homeless, or
   - a student who has an intense interest within a field.

3. Research performance tasks as an element of the nomination and/or identification of students for gifted and talented services. Select two tasks that can be completed within 20 minutes in an elementary classroom

under the supervision of a classroom teacher. Explain why you chose to implement the tasks and what information they are likely to reveal.

Extensions

1. Conduct research on two different quantitative or qualitative assessments to be included in the criteria for entrance into either a STEM magnet high school or an elementary magnet school for highly gifted learners. Write a 500-word abstract in which you discuss the reliability and validity of the assessments and a process for creating local norms.

2. Visit the National Association for Gifted Children website (http://www. nagc.org) or the Davidson Institute (http://www.davidsongifted.org) to identify states with a mandate for the identification of gifted and talented learners. Visit the websites for several states. How do these states' policies deal with identifying gifted students from underrepresented populations? Write a summary statement reflecting what you have learned and list questions and/or concerns you still have regarding this issue. What recommendations, if any, might you make for your own state policy?

3. Interview the gifted and talented coordinator at two school districts of similar size and demographics. Write a two- to four-page paper in which you briefly explain each protocol for the identification of students for services. Identify the strengths of each as well as areas for possible improvement of the protocol.

Additional Readings

Castellano, J. A., & Frazier, A. D. (Eds.). (2011). *Special populations in gifted education: Understanding our most able students from diverse backgrounds.* Waco, TX: Prufrock Press.

Harmon, D. (2004). Improving test performance among culturally diverse gifted students. *Understanding Our Gifted, 16*(4), 18–21. Retrieved from http://www.davidsongifted.org/db/Articles_id_10477.aspx

Little, S. F., & Kaesberg, M. A. (2011). Increasing the eligibility of Title I students for gifted education programs: Pilot study using the Kingore Observation Inventory. *Gifted Education Press Quarterly, 25*(3), 9–14. Retrieved from http://www.giftededpress.com/GEPQSUMMER2011.pdf

Peterson, J. S. (2011). A counselor's perspective on parenting for high potential. In J. L. Jolly, D. J. Treffinger, T. F. Inman, & J. F. Smutny (Eds.), *Parenting gifted children: The authoritative guide from the National Association for Gifted Children* (pp. 525–538). Waco, TX: Prufrock Press.

Schurr, S. (2012). *Authentic assessment: Active, engaging product and performance measures.* Westerville, OH: Association for Middle Level Education.

Smutny, J. F., Haydon, K. P., Bolaños, O., & Danley, G. E. (2012). *Discovering and developing talents in Spanish-speaking students.* Thousand Oaks, CA: Corwin Press.

VanTassel-Baska, J. L. (Ed.). (2008). *Alternative assessments with gifted and talented students.* Waco, TX: Prufrock Press.

VanTassel-Baska, J., & Stambaugh, T. (Eds.). (2007). Overlooked gems: A national perspective on low-income promising learners. *Proceedings of the National Leadership Conference on Low-Income Promising Learners* (Washington, DC, Apr 24–25, 2006). National Association for Gifted Children and the Center for Gifted Education. Retrieved from http://www.nagc.org/uploadedFiles/Publications/Overlooked%20Gems%20(password%20protected%20-%20gifted).pdf

Tonya

Introduction

Not all gifted students fit a mold or exhibit characteristics found on a list. There are some gifted students who have a creative talent and often find themselves struggling to fit into a society that tends to undervalue their abilities, fails to recognize their conflicts, and provides little assistance in meeting both their cognitive and affective needs, while at the same time, expects them to consistently achieve at high levels (Silverman, 1993). This case explores issues related to identifying a creatively gifted child and providing an academic program, that is both challenging and supportive.

Tonya's Mother

Tonya's mother shared the fact that Tonya was always a different kind of child. When she thinks about raising her daughter, she realizes that Tonya has always been "this way." She is a very imaginative child, full of expression, sometimes has outbursts, and is very dramatic. Her favorite subject is art, where she can manipulate different media to express her ideas. She also likes to write in her journal and has been keeping one ever since she has been able to write. Her mother sometimes gets frustrated when she wants Tonya to finish her homework or her chores because she finds Tonya either in the midst of a project not related to school or play acting in front of a mirror. Tonya's mother creates opportunities for the entire family during weekends, taking them to free concerts, museums, and events that cost little or nothing, hoping to keep Tonya excited and interested about the world around her. Neither parent is surprised Tonya is so different because they both felt this way when they were in school. Tonya's mother has recently seen information on the school website about nominating your child for the gifted program but wonders if she should consider it, since Tonya does not receive all A's on her report card.

Tonya

Tonya is in third grade and doesn't want to be like everyone else. She prefers to write about her thoughts and feelings in her journal. Sometimes, she likes to make up stories about the places she sees and the people she meets. At school, she is often "shushed' for her exuberance when learning about something that really interests her and finds that she has so many more questions than answers. The teacher tells her she is too loud in school. Her classmates tolerate her behavior but only because she is good at solving problems. Tonya likes to spend time observing her classmates and often fantasizes about their lives. She seems to have a hard time paying attention during parts of her school day. Sometimes it is hard for her to move on to another subject, especially if she is involved in a project that interests her. Her grades in school are A's and B's, but her teacher feels that if she paid more attention, she could get all A's. When Tonya watches the news on television at home, she feels badly for children who are poor and have few books to read. She would like to do something to help.

Things to Consider

- *Parents and teachers need to understand the characteristics of gifted children and behaviors associated with those characteristics.*
- *Educators need to provide a learning environment that encourages gifted characteristics and behaviors to be exhibited.*
- *Ongoing and comprehensive procedures must be established for identifying and serving gifted students.*
- *Creatively gifted students may not be identified in some school settings.*

Tonya's Teacher

Tonya's teacher does not always know how to keep Tonya focused and on task in her classroom. Tonya sees things differently from her classmates and often comes up with solutions to problems that would never occur to others in the class. Although she is an excellent writer, she tends to do her best work when writing about creative topics. When she gets excited about a lesson, she can almost become overbearing in her exuberance, jumping up and down and taking over, particularly when a creative project is required. At times, this can be disruptive to her classmates. When it is time for Tonya to return from art class, the teacher has a hard time getting her to refocus on her classwork.

Tonya's teacher recently attended a districtwide in-service about nominating and identifying gifted learners. She thinks back to the shared information and wonders if she should nominate Tonya for the gifted program. She is concerned that Tonya might not know how to behave if she were to be placed in a gifted program.

Discussion Questions

1. What are the characteristics of creatively gifted students? What behaviors do the students exhibit in the classroom as a result? Are they positive or negative?
2. Would you identify Tonya as a creatively gifted student? Why or why not?
3. If you would identify Tonya as a creatively gifted student, how would you help her succeed in English? Math? Social Studies? Science?
4. Is her teacher's concern about Tonya's behavior a valid one? Should behavior limit a student's access to gifted and talented programs? Why or why not?
5. What are ways to engage Tonya in the classroom?
6. How would you respond to the statement "schools aren't creative"?
7. Does culture influence creativity? What forms of creativity do different cultures value most?

Activities

1. Do some teachers dislike personality traits associated with creativity? Do some teachers prefer traits that seem to run counter to creativity, such as conformity and unquestioning acceptance of authority? Is it possible that teachers are extinguishing creative behaviors, perhaps unwittingly? Without training, teachers may not identify such children as gifted. Research one or more issues associated with teachers' perceptions of creative students in their classrooms or survey colleagues in your building to determine if they prefer traits that seem to run counter to creativity. Share your results in a PowerPoint.
2. Create a bumper sticker or billboard emphasizing the need to support creative students in our schools or society. Create a poster-sized version that you can display in your classroom or in the hallway at school.
3. Interview a creative person. Determine what questions you might ask. In what ways might you share what you learned in your interview?
4. Review the website for the Center for Creative Learning at http://www.creativelearning.com and more specifically, the link to "Dear School People" at http://www.creativelearning.com/talent-development/dear-school-people and prioritize your top 10 questions from this list. Add your own, if necessary.
5. Create a comprehensive list of resources and local opportunities for creative kids in your community. Include website and contact information for each activity.

Extensions

1. Research the number of states identifying and serving creatively gifted students. Categorize and construct a chart that demonstrates the elements/features of creativity found in the definitions.

2. Compare various districts' identification procedures for gifted programs. Are creatively gifted students identified and served? If so, determine if a variety of assessments are used and reflect on the attributes (e.g., multiple sources, nonbiased and equitable) provided in *Evidence-Based Practices 2.2.2* and *2.2.3* in the *NAGC Pre-K–Grade 12 Gifted Education Programming Standards* (see Appendix A). Make a list of recommendations for improving identification procedures for the creatively gifted child.

3. How are parents notified about the identification process (refer to Appendix A for *Evidence-Based Practice 2.2.6*)? Develop a plan for notifying parents, especially those whose children are underserved or disadvantaged. Include unique or creative options.

4. Read three articles related to identifying a creatively gifted learner. Write a review of each using the *Evidence-Based Practices* described in *2.1–2.3* in the *NAGC Pre-K–Grade 12 Gifted Education Programming Standards* (see Appendix A) as a basis for analysis.

Additional Readings

Beghetto, R. A. (2008). Creativity enhancement. In J. A. Plucker & C. M. Callahan (Eds.), *Critical issues and practices in gifted education: What the research says* (1st ed., pp. 139–154). Waco, TX: Prufrock Press.

Csikszentmihalyi, M. (1996). *Creativity: Flow and the psychology of discovery and invention.* New York, NY: Harper Perennial.

Davis, G. A. (2004). *Creativity is forever* (5th ed.). Dubuque, IA: Kendall Hunt Publishing.

Hunsaker, S. L., & Callahan, C. M. (1995). Creativity and giftedness: Published instrument uses and abuses. *Gifted Child Quarterly, 39,* 110–114. doi:10.1177/001698629503900207

National Association for Gifted Children. (n.d.). *Celebrate creativity.* Newsletter of the NAGC Creativity Network. Retrieved from http://www.nagc.org/CreativityNetwork.aspx

Piirto, J. (2004). *Understanding creativity.* Scottsdale, AZ: Great Potential Press.

Pink, D. H. (2006). *A whole new mind: Why right-brainers will rule the future.* New York, NY: Penguin.

Starko, A. J. (2010). *Creativity in the classroom: Schools of curious delight* (4th ed.). New York, NY: Routledge.

Sternberg, R. J. (Ed.). (1999). *Handbook of creativity.* New York, NY: Cambridge University Press.

Torrance, E. P. (1979). *The search for satori and creativity.* Buffalo, NY: CreativeEducation Foundation.

Treffinger, D. J. (Ed.). (2004). *Creativity and giftedness.* Thousand Oaks, CA: Corwin Press.

Treffinger, D. J., Schoonover, P. F., & Selby, E. C. (2012). *Educating for creativity and innovation: A comprehensive guide for research-based practice.* Waco, TX: Prufrock Press.

VanTassel-Baska, J. (2004, April). Creativity as an elusive factor in giftedness. *Update Magazine.* Retrieved from http://www.hoagiesgifted.org/creativity_as_elusive_factor.htm

Chapter 4

Making Decisions Related to
Curriculum and Instruction

With various research-based models related to planning curriculum and instruction for gifted learners, it is imperative that evidence-based strategies are implemented to ensure progress toward student learning outcomes. The following cases outline the issues related to planning a comprehensive curriculum that challenges the gifted and talented learner.

Gifted Education Programming Standard 3: Curriculum Planning and Instruction

This standard deals with curriculum planning and instructional strategies in addition to the resources needed for implementation in order to meet the needs of diverse learners (see Appendix A).

Mrs. Lewis

Introduction

One of the most challenging groups of gifted students to reach in terms of educational programming is those living in rural areas. What is it like to be a novice teacher in a midsize rural district and be responsible for meeting the needs of your gifted students knowing you have limited resources?

Mrs. Lewis knows she is accountable for meeting the needs, interests, and abilities of her gifted learners, but that doing so is a daunting task. Follow her progress as she considers adapting a former unit of instruction for her new group of gifted learners.

Mrs. Lewis is currently assigned to teach a second- through fifth-grade resource room for the gifted in a midsize rural school district. She has always been interested in working with gifted children and has almost completed her state-required coursework in this field. She is currently enrolled in an online graduate level course related to instructional strategies and curriculum development for the gifted. She knows that there are curricular implications related to the characteristics of all gifted learners. Although her understanding of teaching gifted children is limited by lack of experience, she is excited about this new position. As a teacher of 5 years, she knows several of her previous students have been gifted and tried to adapt and modify her curriculum and instruction. Now, after several courses in gifted education, she feels a bit more confident in what she is doing.

During her first 2 weeks of school, Mrs. Lewis was surprised to learn that the 16 students placed in her resource room had such a wide range of abilities and interests. She also noted that several of her students lived in the local migrant camp, several did not speak English as their primary language, one student had a learning disability in math, and one had a learning disability in reading. In addition, test scores from the Stanford-Binet Intelligence Scales, Fifth Edition (SB-V), indicate one of her children is highly gifted. She thought she would be able to provide more whole-class instruction and activities for her unit on the Westward Movement, but soon concluded that this would not work with the diverse needs of her learners. Her district does not have the funds to provide any additional materials and she only has access to two computers in her classroom. She now knows that her previous expectation was a misconception and she needs to remodel her current unit of study. She decided to go back to her state standards, district-adopted textbook, and her files of collected resources related to this topic to rethink her unit.

Things to Consider

- *Teachers of the gifted in rural school districts often face insurmountable challenges when it comes to providing adequate resources for their students. The limitations include higher costs, a shortage of resource materials, and a sparse population.*
- *There are numerous models of curriculum differentiation that provide flexibility and choice for the range of individual differences in the classroom. Models such as these show how content, teaching and learning processes, and products can be modified to meet the needs of gifted students.*
- *Learners in classrooms vary in degree by their readiness, interest, and learning profile.*
- *Student motivation to learn is enhanced when teachers respond to individual students' readiness, interests, and learning profiles.*
- *Teachers need to develop and implement a variety of instructional strategies in order to meet the needs of their learners.*

Mrs. Lewis knows that the first thing she needs to do is create a plan for remodeling her unit. She remembered many of the strategies related to differentiating the curriculum and instruction, such as modifying the content, process, product, and learning environment. Yet, she only has experience in developing one unit in her graduate-level gifted coursework. Which instructional approaches, materials, and assessment techniques would best accommodate her learner's needs? Which techniques (e.g., learning contracts, tiered assignments, curriculum compacting, learning stations) would work best with her students and how would she know? Once Mrs. Lewis creates her plan, she is ready to implement her changes. In what ways should she define success? What role will assessment (pre and post) contribute to measuring this success? Mrs. Lewis understands that this will not be an easy task but is eager to begin making appropriate changes to her curriculum.

Discussion Questions

1. Although many of the students in Mrs. Lewis's resource room would benefit from her original unit on the Westward Movement, what aspects of the learner should she take into consideration before remodeling her lessons?

2. Looking at *Standard 3: Curriculum Planning and Instruction* (see Appendix A), which student outcomes are *most important* for Mrs. Lewis to address? Why?

3. What steps does Mrs. Lewis need to consider when remodeling her unit of study?
4. What resources and materials in the field would be helpful in doing so?
5. What classroom management strategies for differentiation work best with gifted students who have a diverse range of abilities and interest?
6. What are the unique learning needs of the highly gifted? Highly gifted and rurally isolated?
7. What assessment strategies should Mrs. Lewis plan? Why? What issues need considering when choosing an assessment strategy?
8. What would happen if funds for resources and materials were not an issue? How might Mrs. Lewis proceed with her plan? What might she do differently?

Activities

1. Develop a chart of steps for a generic plan for remolding any unit of study.
2. Identify the key components of curriculum and techniques for modifications appropriate for gifted learners in rural settings. Make a poster or chart of your findings.
3. Adapt a current lesson or a unit plan in response to a diverse group of gifted learners.
4. Identify other ways rural areas can address the needs of their gifted learners in a list or brochure.

Extensions

1. In what ways might teacher training programs about gifted learners provide more support to teachers working with gifted children in rural settings? Discuss your ideas in a small or large group.
2. Research a myth or myths related to gifted children. Investigate what gave rise to the myth, implications of such a myth, suggestions for debunking the myth, and directions for refocusing the myth. Present your findings in a product of your choice.
3. In *Aiming for Excellence* (Landrum, Callahan, & Shaklee, 2001), it is stated that the "emphasis on equity can lead to opposition toward specialized services offered for some, but not all students." Why might this be true? Share your ideas with a colleague.
4. Research the use of a gap analysis chart to assess to what degree your gifted education plans meet state and national requirements. Complete a gap analysis of current curriculum and revisions needed in your district.

Additional Readings

Colangelo, N., & Davis, G. A. (Eds.). (2002). *Handbook of gifted education* (3rd ed.). Boston, MA: Allyn & Bacon.

Kingore, B. (2004). *Differentiation: Simplified, realistic, and effective.* Austin, TX: Professional Associates.

Luhman, A., & Fundis, R. (1989). *Building academically strong gifted programs in rural schools.* Charleston, WV: ERIC Clearinghouse on Rural Education and Small Schools. (ERIC Accession No. ED308060) Retrieved from http://www.nagc.org/index.aspx?id=179

Roberts, J. L., & Inman, T. F. (2012). *Teacher's survival guide: Differentiating instruction in the elementary classroom.* Waco, TX: Prufrock Press.

Tomlinson, C. A., Kaplan, S. N., Purcell, J. H., Leppien, J. H., Burns, D. E., & Strickland, C. A. (2006a). *The parallel curriculum in the classroom, book 1: Essays for application across the content areas, K–12.* Thousand Oaks, CA: Corwin Press.

Tomlinson, C. A., Kaplan, S. N., Purcell, J. H., Leppien, J. H., Burns, D. E., & Strickland, C. A. (2006b). *The parallel curriculum in the classroom, book 2: Units for application across the content areas, K–12.* Thousand Oaks, CA: Corwin Press.

Tomlinson, C. A., Kaplan, S. N., Renzulli, J. S., Purcell, J., Leppien, J., & Burns, D. (2002). *The parallel curriculum: A design to develop high potential and challenge high-ability learners.* Thousand Oaks, CA: Corwin Press.

Treffinger, D. J. (Ed.). (2009). Demythologizing gifted education [Special issue]. *Gifted Child Quarterly, 53*(4).

VanTassel-Baska, J. (2003). *Curriculum planning and instructional design for gifted learners.* Denver, CO: Love.

Mr. Jackson and Miss Mendoza

Introduction

When teachers begin exploring instructional strategies for differentiation, they may find many options are available. How do teachers know which strategies are more effective for meeting the needs of diverse learners? Seldom does a one-size-fits-all approach work. Providing a rich and engaging learning environment maximizes a teacher's capacity to meet the needs of students. This case follows Mr. Jackson's and Miss Mendoza's decision to implement tiered assignments for a variety of readiness levels, interests, and modes of learning in their classrooms.

The Teachers and the School

Teaching in an urban school with students who have different learning experiences, are from different cultures, and possess a variety of characteristics requires instructional strategies that capitalize upon maximizing potential from every learner. The racial-ethnic makeup consists of 44.2% Black, 39.2% Hispanic, 8.3% multiracial, and 4.5% Asian. More than half of the students are on free and reduced lunch. More than 13% of the students have disabilities. Both Mr. Jackson and Miss Mendoza have a diverse group of learners, including gifted and high-ability students. Presented below are some of their individual needs.

Mr. Jackson

Mr. Jackson is working with his high school students on a social studies unit related to the study of how people create, interact with, and change structures of power, authority, and governance. Mr. Jackson needs to be sure that his goals align with the state and district standards. Three of his students exemplify the diversity found in many urban schools:

> *Juan* is hyperactive and likes to breakdance around the room when the class period ends. He is an audio/visual learner, likes to read, and enjoys excelling and being the "class clown." Although he is excited to start new projects, they don't hold his attention. He is a concrete thinker.
>
> *Crystal* does not feel a connection to school. She is a very intelligent student, but considered a "follower." When she applies herself and attends school, she seems to do very well. Crystal has exhibited strong

reading skills, but does not always complete her work because she is busy helping her parents with her younger siblings at home.

Derek failed to pass the state reading exam twice. He would rather be listening to music than paying attention in class. He seems to learn best with hands-on activities. His reading and writing skills have only slightly improved over the last several years.

Miss Mendoza

Miss Mendoza is working with her elementary students on a literature unit related to the growth and change that each person faces in life, which includes a study of *Charlotte's Web* and *The Bridge to Terabithia*. Miss Mendoza also needs to ensure her goals align with the state and district standards. Her students also reflect the diversity found in Mr. Jackson's class:

Lashonda is the teacher's pet and likes to do things to help in the classroom when asked. She wants to fit in with her classmates. She has a wild imagination and loves to read, but her comprehension skills are below grade level. Lashonda often speaks out in class.

Emmanuel is a very quick learner. School is just "easy" for him and he likes to do well. He has a strong concern about rules and right versus wrong. Classmates see him as a leader. His reading and writing skills are both above grade level. He is an abstract thinker.

Solange wants to be a professional basketball player and doesn't know why he needs to go to school to do well. Although he has a great memory, he has some problems in reading and mathematics and seems to be getting by. He has been identified as having dyslexia.

Mr. Jackson and Miss Mendoza need to prepare lessons to help all of their students focus on the knowledge, skills, and understandings related to the curriculum standards while helping all students succeed. They recall a districtwide workshop presented to them about instructional strategies for differentiation including tiered assignments. Both are willing to explore whether this or other strategies will be helpful to meet the specific learning needs of students in their classrooms.

Things to Consider

- *Learners in classrooms vary in degree by their readiness, interest, and learning profiles.*
- *Student motivation to learn is enhanced when teachers respond to individual students' readiness, interests, and learning profiles.*
- *Teachers need to develop and implement a variety of instructional strategies in order to meet the needs of their learners.*

Discussion Questions

1. How familiar are you to the dilemmas of either classroom? Share personal examples of students with similar problems.
2. What will happen to the various learners in these classrooms if their needs remain unmet?
3. What alternatives do Mr. Jackson and Miss Mendoza have for addressing the needs of their students? Is implementing tiered assignments an option to consider? Why or why not?
4. How do you define "tiering"? How might the elements found in "tiered assignments" be an effective instructional tool for meeting the needs of Mr. Jackson and Miss Mendoza's students? Does the implementation of tiered assignments in a secondary setting differ from implementation in an elementary classroom? Why or why not?
5. What strategies do you use to manage differentiation in your classroom?
6. What role, if any, do administrators have in supporting differentiated instruction?
7. What school and community resources are necessary to support differentiation?

Activities

1. Choose one instructional objective and identify two differentiation strategies you might use to teach the objective to one of the students presented in this case. Write a brief article for the building's newsletter or blog in which you explain the strategies you've chosen and why they are appropriate for your classroom.
2. What are the components of a tiered assignment? What do tiered assignments look like in a classroom? Sound like in a classroom? Create a T-chart or collage to explain your ideas.

3. Develop a preassessment to determine the readiness levels of your students. Use a planning guide to develop a tiered assignment for your classroom. (*Note:* The Tomlinson materials in Additional Readings will facilitate this activity.)

4. After implementing a tiered assignment, reflect on what worked and what didn't. Why? Make changes to your lesson as necessary. Prepare a 10-minute presentation on your experience to share with your colleagues at the next team or grade-level meeting.

5. Create a bulletin board or other appropriate venue in the teacher's workroom for sharing that introduces the strategies related to differentiated instruction, including tiered assignments.

Extensions

1. *Evidence-Based Practices 3.3.1* (see Appendix A) recommends that educators select, adapt, and use a repertoire of instructional strategies and materials. Research various instructional strategies for differentiation. Choose one that is unfamiliar and become an expert about that strategy. Develop a brown-bag lunch workshop to share your expertise with others.

2. Develop a 3–5-minute radio or television commercial to explain the implementation of differentiation strategies in the classroom. Present it to a group.

3. What myths are associated with implementing a differentiated classroom? Create an online myth test to administer to colleagues. Using the results, develop a plan of action to help dispel the most prevalent myths.

4. Review and evaluate at least 10 websites about differentiated instruction. Share your findings with colleagues.

Additional Readings

Association for Supervision and Curriculum Development. (1994). *Challenging gifted learners in the regular classroom.* Alexandria, VA: Author. [Video staff development set]. Available from http://shop.ascd.org

Association for Supervision and Curriculum Development. (1997). *Differentiating instruction.* Alexandria, VA: Author. [Video staff development set]. Available from http://shop.ascd.org

Association for Supervision and Curriculum Development. (2002). *At work in the differentiated classroom.* Alexandria, VA: Author. [Video staff development set]. Available from http://shop.ascd.org

Association for Supervision and Curriculum Development. (2003). *Instructional strategies for the differentiated classroom 1–4*. Alexandria, VA: Author. [Video staff development set]. Available from http://shop.ascd.org

Association for Supervision and Curriculum Development. (2004). *Instructional strategies for the differentiated classroom 5–7*. Alexandria, VA: Author. [Video staff development set]. Available from http://shop.ascd.org

Heacox, D. (2002). *Differentiating instruction in the regular classroom: How to reach and teach all learners, grades 3–12*. Minneapolis, MN: Free Spirit.

Heacox, D. (2009). *Making differentiation a habit: How to ensure success in academically diverse classrooms*. Minneapolis, MN: Free Spirit.

Indiana Department of Education, Office of High Ability Education. (2011). *Tiered curriculum project*. Retrieved from http://www.doe.in.gov/achievement/individualized-learning/tiered-curriculum-project

National Association for Gifted Children. (n.d.). *Hot topic: Differentiation of curriculum and instruction*. Retrieved from http://www.nagc.org/index2.aspx?id=978

Meckstroth, E. A. (1997). *Teaching young gifted children in the regular classroom: Identifying, nurturing, and challenging ages 4–9*. Minneapolis, MN: Free Spirit.

Northey, S. S. (2005). *Handbook on differentiated instruction for middle and high schools*. Larchmont, NY: Eye on Education.

Reis, S. M., & Renzulli, J. S. (2005). *Curriculum compacting: An easy start to differentiating for high-potential students*. Waco, TX: Prufrock Press.

Smutny, J. F., & von Fremd, S. E. (2004). *Differentiating for the young child: Teaching strategies across the content areas, K–3*. Thousand Oaks, CA: Corwin Press.

Tomlinson, C. A. (1995a). Deciding to differentiate instruction in middle school: One school's journey. *Gifted Child Quarterly, 39*(2), 77–87. doi:10.1177/001698629503900204

Tomlinson, C. A. (1995b). *How to differentiate instruction in mixed-ability classrooms: A professional inquiry kit*. Alexandria, VA: ASCD.

Tomlinson, C. A. (1999). *The differentiated classroom: Responding to the needs of all learners*. Alexandria, VA: ASCD.

Tomlinson, C. A., Brimijoin, K., & Narvaez, L. (2008). *The differentiated school: Making revolutionary changes in teaching and learning*. Alexandria, VA: ASCD.

Tomlinson, C. A., & Eidson, C. C. (2003a). *Differentiation in practice: A resource guide for differentiating curriculum, grades K–5*. Alexandria, VA: ASCD.

Tomlinson, C. A., & Eidson, C. C. (2003b). *Differentiation in practice: A resource guide for differentiating curriculum, grades 5–9*. Alexandria, VA: ASCD.

Tomlinson, C. A., & Imbeau, M. B. (2010). *Leading and managing a differentiated classroom*. Alexandria, VA: ASCD.

Tomlinson, C. A., Kaplan, S. N., Purcell, J. H., Leppien, J. H., Burns, D. E., & Strickland, C. A. (2005–2006). *The parallel curriculum in the classroom (Vols. 1–2).* Thousand Oaks, CA: Corwin Press.

Tomlinson, C. A., Kaplan, S. N., Renzulli, J. S., Purcell, J., Leppien, J., & Burns, D. (2002). *The parallel curriculum: A design to develop high potential and challenge high-ability learners.* Thousand Oaks, CA: Corwin Press.

Tomlinson, C. A., & Strickland, C. A. (2005). *Differentiation in practice: A resource guide for differentiating curriculum, grades 9–12.* Alexandria, VA: ASCD.

Winebrenner, S. (2001). *Teaching gifted kids in the regular classroom* (Rev. ed.). Minneapolis, MN: Free Spirit.

Mike, Martha, and Lucy

Introduction

Identification of students from diverse backgrounds or with hidden abilities requires that district personnel consider all input from teachers and parents as well as a variety of data about the student. This case presents three minicase studies of students. It includes perspectives of adults who know the students, as well as data to support and inform campus professionals in the decision-making process.

The following minicases have been used by permission of Jim Coffey, Region 15 Education Service Center, San Angelo, TX.

Mike Guerra, Eighth Grade

Mike's parent has nominated him for gifted and talented services for the past 3 years. His sixth-grade teacher concurred with the nomination, but he was not identified for services at seventh grade. The current teachers did not nominate him. His mother states:

> Miguel began to put words together when he was 2. He spoke much earlier than my other children. He began to read signs and labels on things at the store when he was riding in the shopping basket. He was always asking, "What is this, Mama?" When his Dad was alive, he talked to me about how Miguel always wanted to work on the car with him. He would say "How does this make it go?" You know, wanting to know how things worked. He still likes science stuff. He can fix anything. He likes to read but not all of the books in his classes. He loves science fiction; he calls it "fantasy" and has written some. Last year, he went to Monterey for the summer and worked for my brother in his shop. We have talked about him going to college but I don't see how I can send him with only my income. Maybe if he sees he can do something in the gifted program, he will be more interested in college.

Mike's scores and data are as follows:

SAGES II		
Math/Science	Quotient 122	93rd percentile
Language Arts/Social Studies	Quotient 116	86th percentile
Reasoning	Quotient 123	94th percentile
Naglieri Ability Index	126–127	
Portfolio: One poem that had been published in the local weekly newspaper; science fair award for second place on the topic "Offshore Drilling and Impact on Commercial Fishing;" a plan for the development of a classic hot rod magazine to be produced on the Internet. The plan includes the work of other students in the development of the project. Miguel serves as editor and "idea-ist."		

Mike's Teachers' Comments

Language Arts Teacher: "Despite the high overall academic rating, I do not consider Mr. Guerra a particularly promising candidate for advanced programs. He is inconsistent with homework, seemingly preferring to finish the last few pages at the beginning of class, or presenting some other worn-out excuse. He has little interest in my class and makes it perfectly clear by following the lead of several of the other children (I don't consider them 'young men') who want to delay the class and ask questions that do not contribute to the progress of the class." Current grade in class is a B-.

Science Teacher: "Miguel is an outstanding student. His questioning keeps me on my toes all of the time. I am always afraid he is going to ask something I can't answer; it is almost like a game with him. Sometimes he and a couple of friends will stay after class a minute or two just to continue the discussion. I require students to do projects; and Miguel created a model of how a windmill could be used as the primary power supply to drive a pump, using mechanical linkage, to pump water out of an isolated canyon. I think he got the idea from his uncle who lives in Mexico, but the presentation was outstanding. I don't know why I didn't think of nominating him!" Current grade in class is an A.

Social Studies Teacher: "I have known Miguel since seventh grade. I coached him in football and in the required off-season conditioning. He was a quick learner on the field, although lacking in speed to play receiver. He tried very hard and worked well up to the time he injured his knee. His best game was against McMurtry, but he was playing injured then as well. I doubt that he will return to football in ninth grade. He was in my Texas History class and I think he may have had a reading problem. He enjoyed oral presentations and did well when he was able to work with some of his friends. I think that all of them might have had some sort of learning problem individually, but together they made a great team." Current grade in class is an A.

Math Teacher: "Mike is a quiet student. Most of my students are pre-AP. While we do not do a lot different for the Pre-AP students, they are students who have been in gifted classes for some time and work well together. Mike may not fit in well with them. He has a strong analytical mind, but doesn't speak up in class very often. The other students always seem to get the answer before he does." Current grade in class is a B+.

Things to Consider

- *Parents offer a different perspective of their child based on nonschool activities and interests.*
- *School personnel making decisions about the identification for services must be well-grounded in the pedagogy of gifted education.*
- *Identification for services and the services themselves must match the needs of the gifted child and/or young adult.*

Martha Lawrence, Ninth Grade

Martha's social studies teacher and her parents nominated Martha for gifted and talented services. Portions of her parents' comments include:

> "There is much evidence to support placing Martha in advanced classes. She was enrolled in Waverly Academy from Pre-K until the end of eighth grade. She was always considered an outstanding student by the teachers and was a stand out in sports. She played volleyball, field hockey, and tennis. She responded very well to coaching and invariably worked well with the less talented girls. Now that she is entering public school, she needs to be with others of her experience and ability. Both of her sisters were in gifted programs and have done well in college."

Martha's scores and data are as follows:

SAGES-II		
Math/Science	Quotient 99	48th percentile
Language Arts/Social Studies	Quotient 108	70th percentile
Reasoning	Quotient 101	52nd percentile
Naglieri Ability Index	114	82nd percentile
Portfolio: A cookbook done with her sister and mother consisting of family recipes and photographs; a scrapbook of family vacations; grade cards from Waverly Academy.		

Martha's Teachers' Comments

Language Arts Teacher: "Martha works very hard and is a popular straight-A student. She has a particular affinity for poetry and has written some very astute material that has been submitted to several local publications. She is involved in cheerleading, and is manager for the boys' basketball team. She seems overwhelmed and intimidated by intellectual discussion. She is very concerned about how others perceive her; however, most of the others see her as smart and capable." Current grade in class is an A-.

Science Teacher: "Martha has taken the required courses and did well with them. She is a straight-A student and very pleasant." Current grade in class is an A.

Social Studies Teacher: "Martha is a joy to have in the class. She is prepared and does well on the tests. She is not a discipline problem and volunteers to tutor others in the class when she finishes her work early. She will be a freshman cheerleader next year and we expect great things from that squad." Current grade in class is a B+ ("I think she can do better than this; she just has had a few low grades on her projects".)

Math Teacher: "Martha is always prepared for class. She seems to learn very easily, but tends to avoid advanced work. I think that she is capable of the work; it is just that she is very busy with cheerleading and sports. Her family has very high expectations of her, and she seems determined to attain the levels expected of her." Current grade in class is an A-.

Lucy Greenwell, 10th Grade

The assistant principal nominated Lucy for gifted and talented services. Lucy's parents are divorced, so nominations were sought from each of them. Her mother did not return the form, but her father did. Lucy's father comments:

"I read to Lucy from the time she was born until about a year or 2 ago. When she was small, it was just something I did; later it got to be something we did together. She would read books into a tape recorder for me to take on trips and I would do the same for her. It got to the point that I read textbooks for her, and she said she learned faster that way. I don't know if she is gifted, but she is certainly very bright and has a great desire to learn. I worry about that. Last year, she and a friend had a plan to spend the summer in Merida, Mexico, to study Spanish and art. I didn't want her to go and we had a big fight about it. She didn't go and I think that she is still upset with me about it."

Lucy's Assistant Principal's Comments

"I think that Lucy is a great candidate for gifted services. While she does not have all of the characteristics of the gifted learner that appear on the list we got from central office, she has some interesting ones. She is very bright. In those courses that she is interested in, she challenges the teacher with her knowledge of the content. Her grades in Advanced History and Advanced Language Arts are always near the top of the class, certainly in the top 5%. In her other classes, she is either adequate or bright enough to know that she can keep quiet and stay out of trouble. She has not had as many discipline referrals this year as last. The biggest problem I have had with her was the body piercing incident and that cleared up when the infection did."

SAGES-II		
Math/Science	Quotient 115	84th percentile
Language Arts/Social Studies	Quotient 134	99th percentile
Reasoning	Quotient 137	99th percentile
Naglieri Ability Index	130	98th percentile

Portfolio: Photo album of "Life at Night," a compilation of photographs taken by Lucy on weekends at the mall and friends' houses; first draft of a novel about a girl who learns that a family of great apes at the zoo has learned language from humans by listening and watching them and then plan an escape, notes for her study on Gypsies.

Lucy's Teachers' Comments

Language Arts Teacher: "Dealing with Lucy has been a task this year. Although she loves to read, she does not love to read her assignments. She constantly wants to distract the class by discussing some extracurricular reading she has done. She reads the *San Antonio Express-News*, and when they did a series on

Latin American literature, she announced that 'Perhaps we should read Isabel Allende and Sandra Cisneros since they represented a coming trend in literature in Texas.' I could tell that her comments made several of the students uncomfortable. Generally, she is compliant in class and her work is average to above average on her 'good day.' I am concerned about her increasing erratic behavior as evidenced by the piercing incident earlier in the year." Current grade in class is an A-.

Science Teacher: "Lucy is a challenge in class. She is always eager to learn and to bring into class information that she gathered in her wide-ranging reading outside of class. Her questions inspired us all to examine the interdependence of the biosystems when she read something about planned destruction of the rainforest by large global interests. So, I restructured my instruction a little and expanded what I intended to do. It got bigger than I thought it would. By the end of the year, everyone was ready to picket the United Nations or someone because of the study we did. Lucy was a leader in that one." Current grade in class is an A.

Social Studies Teacher: "I think that the thing that impresses me the most about Lucy is that a young woman her age can make the connections that she does. She has the characteristics of a good athlete in that I can explain a concept one time and she runs with it after that. I have been tempted to allow her to teach certain concepts to the students because she understands major ideas so well. She draws the ideas out on her paper and explains them to the girl that sits next to her. I thought they were just passing notes until I picked up several and saw what was happening. Now, I have moved them to the back of the class so they won't be as disruptive and allowed this tutoring to go on. On a side note, she became very interested in Gypsies last year. This interest led to some problems that became well known all over school and contributed to the health problems she experienced."

Math Teacher: "I enjoy having Lucy in class. I don't think that she is gifted. She has . . . " (Form was turned in incomplete.)

Discussion Questions

1. In what ways could you evaluate the data and narratives of Mike, Martha, and Lucy? For example, will you place emphasis on test scores, teacher input, or parent input?
2. How important is class participation in relation to identification for services? Support your answer.
3. What other resources could be used to help identify and/or accommodate the learning needs of Mike? Of Martha? Of Lucy?
4. According to NAGC's position paper, "Redefining Giftedness for a New Century: Shifting the Paradigm" 2008a; (http://www.nagc.org/index.aspx?id=6404) in what domains would Mike, Lucy, and Martha be considered gifted? What factors might enhance or inhibit the development and expression of each student's abilities?

Activities

1. These cases do not include the students' perspectives. From personal experience and/or Additional Readings, add to one of the cases from the perspective of one of the students.

2. Create an identification profile or matrix that includes the information from one of the students. Examples may be found on surrounding districts' websites, or at the state department for gifted education in your state.

3. Define the characteristics of giftedness exhibited by the three students (See http://www.nagc.org/WhatisGiftedness.aspx for various definitions of giftedness). Using a graphic organizer, compare and contrast the students' characteristics based on the information given.

4. Create a dialogue of talking points for speaking with the counselor, administrator, and the students' parents about what services will or will not be offered.

Extensions

1. Write a brief case study of three students in your school who have not been identified for services. Create a list of questions that could be used for analysis of each case.

2. Create a unit of study for your three students or any gifted or above average students.

3. Use *Standard 3: Curriculum Planning and Instruction* (see Appendix A) to develop a 3-hour professional development session for your campus based on the needs of one of the students in the case study you created in question number one. If appropriate, present it to your faculty.

4. Research best practices for *Standard 3: Curriculum Planning and Instruction* related to *Evidence-Based Practices* (see Appendix A). Develop one activity that would facilitate a practice in one of your students' classroom. Use the dialogue from Activity 4 as a guide.

5. Select a participant to role-play at least one of your student's parents with the counselor, principal, and/or the gifted and talented coordinator in a discussion to determine services.

Additional Readings

Brighton, C. M., & Moon, T. R. (2007, November). *Two decades of research on differentiation: What do we now know?* Presentation at the National Association for Gifted Children Annual Professional Development Conference,

Minneapolis, MN. Retrieved from http://nrcgtuva.org/presentations/ TwoDecadesofResearch_CMBTRM2007.pdf

Colangelo, N., Kerr, B., Christensen, P., & Maxey, J. (2004). A comparison of gifted underachievers and gifted high achievers. In S. M. Reis (Series Ed.) & S. M. Moon (Vol. Ed.), *Essential readings in gifted education series: Vol. 8. Social/emotional issues, underachievement, and counseling of gifted and talented students* (pp. 119–132). Thousand Oaks, CA: Corwin Press.

Coleman, L. J., & Cross, T. L. (2005). *Being gifted in school: An introduction to development, guidance, and teaching* (2nd ed.). Waco, TX: Prufrock Press.

Galbraith, J., & Delisle, J. (2011). *The gifted teen survival guide: Smart, sharp, and ready for (almost) anything* (4th ed.). Minneapolis, MN: Free Spirit.

Hoover-Schultz, B. (2005). Gifted underachievement: Oxymoron or educational enigma? In S. K. Johnsen & J. Kendrick (Eds.), *Teaching strategies in gifted education* (pp. 127–136). Waco, TX: Prufrock Press. Retrieved from http:// www.mcrgroup.org/bogota/Resources/Articles/Schultz.pdf

Johnsen, S. K. (Ed.). (2011). *Identifying gifted students: A practical guide* (2nd ed.). Waco, TX: Prufrock Press.

Johnsen, S. K., Haensly, P. A., Ryser, G. R., & Ford, R. F. (2002). Changing general education classroom practices to adapt for gifted students. *Gifted Child Quarterly, 46*(1), 45–63. doi:10.1177/001698620204600105

Johnsen, S., Haensly, P., Ryser, G., & McIntosh, J. (1994). *Project Mustard Seed: Application for continuation grant under Javits Gifted and Talented Students Education Program*. Washington, DC: U. S. Office of Education.

Kearney, K. (1992). Life in the asynchronous family. *Understanding Our Gifted, 4*(6), 1, 8–12. Available from http://www.hoagiesgifted.org/asynchronous. htm

National Association for Gifted Children. (n.d.). *Meeting the needs of high ability and high potential learners in the middle grades*. Retrieved from http://www. nagc.org/index.aspx?id=400

Slocumb, P. D., & Payne, R. K. (2000). *Removing the mask: Giftedness in poverty*. Highlands, TX: Aha! Process.

Tomlinson, C. A. (1995). *Gifted learners and the middle school: Problem or promise?* [ERIC EC Digest E535]. Retrieved from http://www.nagc.org/index. aspx?id=150

Tomlinson, C. A. (1999). *The differentiated classroom: Responding to the needs of all learners*. Alexandria, VA: ASCD.

VanTassel-Baska, J., & Stambaugh, T. (2005). Challenges and possibilities for serving gifted learners in the regular classroom. *Theory Into Practice, 44,* 211–217. doi:10.1207/s15430421tip4403_5

Chapter 5

---◯---

Creating Safe and Productive Learning Environments

Safe and productive learning environments are those that support emotional and intellectual growth. Educators must create learning environments for gifted individuals that foster cultural understanding, safety and emotional well-being, positive social interactions, and active engagement. In addition, educators of the gifted must foster environments in which diversity is not just understood but valued. The following cases reflect how educators shape the environment to encourage independence, motivation, and self-advocacy of gifted and talented students.

Gifted Education Programming Standard 4: Learning Environments

This standard addresses the need to create safe learning environments that support the cognitive, social and emotional needs of gifted and talented learners emphasizing a variety of competencies in areas such as leadership and communication (see Appendix A)

Raul

Introduction

The United States is an increasingly diverse nation. Preparing the education professional to recognize and respond to the needs of students from diverse, at-risk populations is critical to student achievement, post-secondary success, and ultimately, the future of the United States.

For diverse learners living in poverty, the issue takes on a special poignancy. The cruel reality is that these learners are most likely to receive instruction from teachers with the least training in schools with the most severely limited resources. Sadly, all too often, students in these circumstances are victims of the soft bigotry of low expectations where little is expected, and little is encouraged.

Although the Hispanic/Latino population is the largest and fastest growing minority in the United States (U.S. Census Bureau, 2003), many educators remain unaware of diversity's impact on their students and classrooms. Cultural competency, the ability of people to successfully interact with and understand others whose culture differs from their own, is an increasingly important skill for all educators. For educators of the gifted, cultural competency is the skill set necessary to support and assist in the identification of underrepresented populations. Gifted learners from diverse backgrounds may need complex support in which the hidden rules of culture are acknowledged and respected. As education professionals, it is our obligation to ensure these systems exist.

Raul's case study introduces the professional to a high school student who appears to lack the motivation and engagement to attend class.

The town of Maryville, located in the southern part of the state, was once a stable community. In recent years, several factories have closed, and the unemployment rate has increased to 23%. Once a town with a population of more than 23,000, Maryville now counts 18,502 residents and a K–12 school population of 4,728. The district reports to the state that the students are 3% Asian, 9% Black, 16% Latino, and 72% White. The school's population consists of 18% Limited English Proficient students, 28% special education students, and 72% recipients of free and reduced lunch. Resources are almost nonexistent; technology and textbooks are outdated, and the roof leaks. Administrators spend the majority of their time addressing disciplinary, facility, and budgetary issues. The district has not made adequate yearly progress (AYP) in either math or reading in any of the buildings, and school restructuring within 2 years is almost certain. Class sizes are large, and morale among the staff has remained low since the third attempt to pass a referendum, in which a proposal to raise taxes to fund building repairs failed.

Raul's parents are immigrants who work several jobs to provide for their five children. His father works during the day at a meat packing plant, sleeps a few hours, and then cleans offices for a local bank. Raul's mother cleans rooms at a local motel before heading to her other job at a fast food franchise. When she arrives home, late at night, she is exhausted and often collapses on the couch. Each morning Raul, age 15, helps his siblings of 5, 9, 11, and 12 years get ready for school. After school, he supervises homework, prepares supper, and puts the younger siblings to bed before beginning his homework. Raul has few friends and prefers to eat his lunch alone. Raul's parents cannot afford to miss work to care for the children if they are ill. Therefore, he stays home from school if his siblings are ill or running late. Consequently, he misses a lot of school and is tardy more often than not.

Things to Consider

- *Culture impacts students every moment of every day.*
- *Family and community are core values in the Hispanic/Latino culture.*
- *Hispanic/Latino families value self-sufficiency and are unlikely to request or depend on assistance from outside of the family.*
- *Attendance issues are often more complex than they appear.*
- *Generational poverty impacts what students think about themselves, school, and aspirations for the future.*
- *"What we don't know we make up" (Donna Ford).*

Raul's math teacher, Mrs. Smith, is tired. Her expectations are low, and she has grown accustomed to students sleeping through class. She rarely wakes them, circumventing confrontation and dealing with the shortage of textbooks. Although Raul likes math, he is often unable to complete his homework. He has no calculator and too much pride to borrow one. Mrs. Smith believes Raul listens in class but can't understand why he doesn't turn in his assignments. After Raul scores in the 95th percentile on the state Graduation-Required Assessment for Diploma (GRAD) math test, she reads his cumulative file. Much to her surprise, Mrs. Smith discovers a history of high test scores, low attendance, and poor grades. Armed with the data, she meets with the dean to support Raul's placement in next year's honors math class. When she learns Raul has refused to register for the class, Mrs. Smith becomes aggravated and determines that it's the last time she will spend time advocating for a student.

Discussion Questions

1. Why is Raul reluctant to register for the honors math class? What environmental factors may have influenced his decision?
2. *Standard 4: Learning Environment* (see Appendix A) references personal competence. Students with gifts and talents demonstrate growth in personal competence and dispositions for exceptional academic and creative productivity. Does Raul exhibit self-awareness, self-advocacy, self-efficacy, confidence, motivation, resilience, independence, curiosity, and/or risk taking? What evidence supports your decision?
3. Would Raul benefit from identification as a gifted learner? Is assessment of potential appropriate or inappropriate for high school students? Explain why.
4. Is Raul at risk? Why or why not? What systems of support would benefit Raul?
5. Cultural competency is the ability of people to successfully interact with and understand others whose culture differs from their own. Does Mrs. Smith display cultural competency in her understanding of Raul's situation? Why or why not?

Activities

1. Research the concept of a "Forced Choice Dilemma" and prepare a short presentation to share with your colleagues.
2. With colleagues, role-play a conversation with Raul's parents.
3. Research organizations that support promising learners, like Raul, who come from impoverished environments. Create a list of local resources for at-risk students.

Extensions

1. Research *Standard 6: Professional Development* (see Appendix A) and design a cultural competency workshop for Mrs. Smith and the teachers at her school.
2. Select a journal article on diverse gifted learners to read and discuss with your PLC. Identify questions for the discussion.
3. Create a gap analysis tool that building-level teams can use to identify culturally sensitive professional development needs.

Additional Readings

Castellano, J. A. (2003). *Special populations in gifted education: Working with diverse gifted learners.* Boston, MA: Allyn & Bacon.

Castellano, J. A., & Frazier, A. D. (Eds.). (2011). *Special populations in gifted education: Understanding our most able students from diverse backgrounds.* Waco, TX: Prufrock Press.

Dixon, F. A., & Moon, S. M. (Eds.). (2006). *The handbook of secondary gifted education.* Waco, TX: Prufrock Press.

Ford, D. Y., & Harris, J. J. (1999). *Multicultural gifted education.* New York, NY: Teachers College Press.

Ford, D. Y., & Milner, H. R. (2005). *Teaching culturally diverse gifted students.* Waco, TX: Prufrock Press.

Slocumb, P. D., & Payne, R. K. (2000). *Removing the mask: Giftedness in poverty.* Highlands, TX: Aha! Process.

Smith-Adcock, S., Daniels, M. H., Lee, S. M., Villalba, J. A., & Indelicato, N. A. (2006). Culturally responsive school counseling for Hispanic/Latino students and families: The need for bilingual school counselors. *Professional School Counseling, 10*(1), 92–101. (Accession No. 22814977)

Valencia, R. R. (2010). *Dismantling contemporary deficit thinking: Educational thought and practice.* New York, NY: Routledge.

VanTassel-Baska, J. L. (Ed.). (2010). *Patterns and profiles of promising learners from poverty.* Waco, TX: Prufrock Press.

VanTassel-Baska, J., & Stambaugh, T. (Eds.). (2007). Overlooked gems: A national perspective on low-income promising learners. *Proceedings of the National Leadership Conference on Low-Income Promising Learners* (Washington, DC, Apr 24–25, 2006). National Association for Gifted Children and the Center for Gifted Education. Retrieved from http://www.nagc.org/uploadedFiles/Publications/Overlooked%20Gems%20(password%20protected%20-%20gifted).pdf

Rebecca

Introduction

When students feel their experiences, cultural heritage, language, and values are recognized and supported in the curriculum and instruction received at school, they are more likely to demonstrate the motivation, effort, and attitude for becoming high achievers. This curricular relevance applies not only to minority groups, but also to majority cultures living in depressed areas where norms and beliefs are not necessarily valued in school, and vice-versa (Olszewski-Kubilius & Clarenbach, 2012).

This case introduces the education professional to the curricular impact and relevance of poverty on low-income, high-ability students and their families. For many of these students, access to a challenging and appropriate education is threatened by a school culture of low-expectations, apathy, and identification models that do not capitalize on the students' unique cultural experiences and strengths.

Naomi was 16 when she became a single mother and dropped out of school. She had been an average student, quiet and cautious in class. Naomi's classmates and teachers did not know her very well or offer advice on options for staying in school. With the help of her "Aunties," she managed to raise her daughter, Rebecca, as a happy and healthy child. When Naomi went to work, her Aunties took turns rocking her baby, sharing stories and songs. When Rebecca was old enough to hold a sewing needle, her Aunties taught her to sew and bead. During their long walks in the woods, Rebecca was introduced to the names of trees and plants and to their medicinal utilities. Although she lived in poverty, Rebecca was endowed with a rich heritage and a deep respect for nature.

At 5, Rebecca was enrolled in kindergarten. The school was in Touren, a town 30 miles north of the Indian reservation on which she lived. Each morning she took the long bus ride to school with her older twin cousins, John and Seth. They were jovial, and sitting with the group made her feel proud, strong, and safe. They shared stories about the "funny White kids" in their classes, and everyone smiled when Rebecca talked about becoming a scientist or a doctor. By the end of second grade, Rebecca excelled in all subjects and read every book on plants and animals in the school library. Having come from poverty, as well as being from a minority group considered to be among the lowest achieving student groups, Naomi was proud of her daughter's progress.

Naomi hoped Rebecca would be among the first from the reservation to attend college, especially with all of the struggles Rebecca witnessed her cousins experience at school. When Rebecca was in fifth grade, her cousins stopped riding the bus due to a series of fights. Their parents gratefully accepted an older cousin's offer of the boys' transportation to school. Furthermore, at the age of 16, both boys were struggling readers and failing several classes. Before class one day, John answered a classmate's racial slur with a punch, and the school expelled him. The following day, Seth dropped out of school in protest and no one questioned his decision. The following year, their sister Sarah joined them at home. Although a talented artist, she too struggled to read.

Today, Rebecca is in the seventh grade and is the only American Indian student in her classes. She has no friends at school and sits alone on the long bus ride to and from middle school. She pretends not to hear her classmate's comments about her long braids and odd clothing. What once seemed like a safe haven for Rebecca now feels like pure isolation.

Rebecca's teachers regard her as an average to above-average student. She is compliant, but her work is unremarkable. She answers dutifully when called upon, but never volunteers in her classes. If she has questions, she approaches her teachers after class. Her teachers are unaware of her feelings of isolation, or her dream of becoming a scientist or doctor.

Things to Consider

- *Each of the 565 American Indian tribes in the United States has a unique tradition, language, and culture. American Indians are more likely to be geographically isolated and experience generational poverty than any other minority group in the United States.*

- *American Indians remain among the lowest achieving student groups in the United States.*

- *The characteristics of high-ability American Indian students may differ significantly from the characteristics and behaviors typically associated with gifted children.*

- *Educators who provide a culturally responsive learning environment encourage students to exhibit gifted characteristics and behaviors.*

- *American Indians are unlikely to draw attention to themselves, and typically value family and community above individual accomplishments.*

Rebecca's fourth-period science class is her favorite class of the day. She likes her teacher, Miss Elkin, and loves learning about plants and animals. The similarities and differences in their cell structure intrigue Rebecca. She is excited when Miss Elkin announces a project worth 60% of the fall quarter grade. The students are to collect, press, and mount 35 leaf specimens. They have been instructed to label each specimen with the common and scientific names. The collections are due next week and Rebecca hopes Miss Elkin will appreciate her effort to include many extra specimens with information about their medicinal values.

Although typically silent in class, Rebecca has recently begun to participate in discussions by volunteering information about where particular specimens are located. Miss Elkin is surprised at Rebecca's enthusiasm for the project and the depth of her knowledge. She has asked Rebecca to assist several of her classmates with their projects.

Discussion Questions

1. In what ways might poverty and minority status affect the way in which the typical characteristics of a gifted student are exhibited? Does Rebecca demonstrate some of the characteristics of a gifted learner? Why or why not? If Rebecca is gifted, why might educators and administrators in her school district overlook her? Explain your position.
2. Why are American Indian children disproportionately underidentified as gifted and talented?
3. How does generational poverty differ from situational poverty? Describe how each factor impacts gifted learners.
4. How are reading difficulties connected to poverty? In relation to this connection, what are the implications for American Indians and other minority groups?
5. In what ways can Miss Elkin nurture and support Rebecca's interest in science?

Activities

1. Prepare an 8–10-minute presentation on a talent development model to share with your colleagues. As a part of your presentation, discuss the potential for improving achievement of promising low-income learners.
2. Write a 250-word op-ed calling for a task force or working group to explore the feasibility of creating a pilot program for the local school district. The pilot program should focus on the needs of low-income, high-ability learners in or outside of school.
3. Working with a colleague, identify three films that portray low-income, high-ability minority students as the main character. Plan an informal

discussion with your colleague, in which you review the content of the films and discuss how they promote or dispel stereotypes about low-income, high-ability, or minority status learners. Present salient points in your discussion to the colleague.

4. Prepare a 5–10 minute presentation on the HOPE Scale to your colleagues. Discuss how its use can help identify diverse populations.

Extensions

1. Create a synthesis of articles on the nature and development of psychosocial characteristics in low-income promising learners or gifted American Indian children. Submit your synthesis to a colleague for feedback, and then submit for publication to one of the following: *Journal of the Education of the Gifted, Twice-Exceptional Newsletter, Gifted Child Today, Gifted Child Quarterly*, or other appropriate venues.

2. Create a teacher's guide for a film to be used in a classroom setting to help students gain insight into the challenges and opportunities faced by low-income, high-ability, minority learners.

3. *Standard 4: Learning Environments Evidence-Based Practices 4.1.2* (see Appendix A) references personal competence for gifted learners. The standard requires educators to provide opportunities for self-exploration, development and pursuit of interests, and development of identities supportive of achievement (e.g., through mentors and role models). Design a 5-year plan for Miss Elkin and others to nurture and support Rebecca's interest in science. Make a list of recommendations to share with Rebecca and her mother.

Additional Readings

Castellano, J. A. (2003). *Special populations in gifted education: Working with diverse gifted learners.* Boston, MA: Allyn & Bacon.

Castellano, J. A., & Frazier, A. D. (Eds.). (2011). *Special populations in gifted education: Understanding our most able students from diverse backgrounds.* Waco, TX: Prufrock Press.

Dixon, F. A., & Moon, S. M. (Eds.). (2006). *The handbook of secondary gifted education.* Waco, TX: Prufrock Press.

Fisher, T. J. (2007). Identifying and teaching gifted Native American students. *Understanding Our Gifted, 20*(1), 3–6.

Ford, D.Y. (2011). *Multicultural gifted education* (2nd ed.). Waco, TX: Prufrock Press.

Gay, G. (2010). *Culturally responsive teaching: Theory, research, and practice* (2nd ed.). New York, NY: Teachers College Press.

Gentry, M., & Fugate, C. M. (2012). Gifted Native American students: Underperforming, under-identified, and overlooked. *Psychology in the Schools, 49*, 631–646. doi:10.1002/pits.21624 (Also available from http://www.geri.education.purdue.edu/PDF%20Files/GENTRY/Gentry Fugate2012.pdf)

Good, C. (2012). Reformulation of the talent equation: Implications for gifted students' sense of belonging and achievement. In R. F. Subotnik, A. Robinson, C. M. Callahan, & E. J. Gubbins (Eds.), *Malleable minds: Translating insights from psychology and neuroscience to gifted education* (pp. 37–54). Storrs: The University of Connecticut National Research Center on the Gifted and Talented.

National Association for Gifted Children. (n.d.). *Meeting the needs of high ability and high potential learners in the middle grades* [Position statement]. Retrieved from http://www.nagc.org/index.aspx?id=400

Raborn, J. (2002, Fall). Challenging schools' expectations of Native American students. *The National Research Center on the Gifted and Talented Newsletter*, 9–11. Retrieved from http://www.gifted.uconn.edu/nrcgt/newsletter/fall02/fall023.html

Slocumb, P. D., & Payne, R. K. (2000a). Identifying and nurturing the gifted poor. *Principal: The New Diversity, 79*(5), 28–32. Retrieved from http://www.nagc.org/index.aspx?id=656

Slocumb, P. D., & Payne, R. K. (2000b). *Removing the mask: Giftedness in poverty.* Highlands, TX: Aha! Process.

Stambaugh, T., & Chandler, K. L. (2012). *Effective curriculum for underserved gifted students.* Waco, TX: Prufrock Press.

Valencia, R. R. (2010). *Dismantling contemporary deficit thinking: Educational thought and practice.* New York, NY: Routledge.

VanTassel-Baska, J., & Stambaugh, T. (Eds.). (2007). Overlooked gems: A national perspective on low-income promising learners. *Proceedings of the National Leadership Conference on Low-Income Promising Learners* (Washington, DC, Apr 24–25, 2006). National Association for Gifted Children and the Center for Gifted Education. Retrieved from http://www.nagc.org/uploadedFiles/Publications/Overlooked%20Gems%20(password%20protected%20-%20gifted).pdf

VanTassel-Baska, J. L. (Ed.). (2010). *Patterns and profiles of promising learners from poverty.* Waco, TX: Prufrock Press.

Ingrid

Introduction

Young gifted children may reach developmental milestones earlier than anticipated and enter school with a skill set that requires early and ongoing differentiated learning opportunities. This case study introduces the education professional to a parent's perspective and the conflict that may occur when student needs are neither recognized nor supported.

Ingrid's Parents

When our daughter Ingrid was born, we were overjoyed. She was our first child and perfect in every way. We had assumed our newborn would sleep most of the day and night; we soon learned our daughter had other ideas. She wasn't fussy, just alert, and from the beginning seemed to track everyone with her eyes and everything around her. Her growth was steady and her well-baby check-ups unremarkable. Although she seemed to sleep less than other newborns, our pediatrician assured us she was fine.

We provided Ingrid with the usual assortment of stuffed animals, board books, and developmentally appropriate toys. She seemed to listen intently to the stories we read to her and would often flip through the pages of board books when one was within reach. She enjoyed listening to her father play the piano and we were pleased she shared our love of music.

When the weather grew cold, Ingrid was 9 months old so I took her to a shoe store to be fitted for her first "real" pair of shoes. They were a sturdy white leather, and I was certain they would provide the support needed for Ingrid's first steps. That evening when her father came home Ingrid pointed to her feet and proudly announced, "new shoes." Her language skills seemed to develop overnight and by 12 months, she followed simple directions, and asked as well as answered questions. After what seemed an eternity, she walked without aid at 14 months. Delighted with her new ability, she walked into the kitchen and began to play with the brightly colored letter magnets on the refrigerator door.

Ingrid's fascination with letters continued. She had learned to sing the alphabet by listening to a lullaby tape at bedtime; and at the age of 2, she could alphabetically arrange the magnetic letters on the refrigerator door.

Ingrid started preschool at the age of 3, and at conference time her teachers described her as curious, well-behaved, but somewhat distant from the other children. They observed that she was generally cautious and seemed content to sit alone and "read" books or play with puzzles. She was the only child who hadn't slid down the classroom slide and they worked daily to coax her to do so.

Ingrid seemed disappointed by kindergarten. She thought she would learn new and exciting things when she attended "real school." At dinner, she complained about the "silly" questions her teacher asked. She was a self-taught reader interested in chapter books and not in learning letter sounds. At conference time, we learned that Ingrid rarely contributed to class discussion, speaking only when called upon.

Things to Consider

- *Parents of gifted children are often the first to notice behaviors that differ from other children. They can provide valuable information to educators about their children.*
- *When educators and parents communicate and collaborate with each other they are more likely to provide the systems of support that gifted learners require.*
- *Young gifted learners may require systems of support before formal identification and gifted programs are available to them.*

First grade was a better year for Ingrid. Her teacher recognized Ingrid's advanced abilities, adding challenging spelling words and higher level reading materials to her curriculum. Ingrid would often stay after school to talk with her teacher about an interesting book she had read or an article in *Newsweek* magazine. She walked to school with a third-grade neighbor, and we were relieved that Ingrid finally had a friend.

Although second-grade classroom work offered few challenges, Ingrid enjoyed piano lessons, scouting, trips to the library, and the concerts we attended on occasion. At some point, we realized she had learned how to sit quietly in class and to appear as if she were listening. She completed her daily worksheets quickly, hoping to earn extra reading time during her school day. Her worksheets were sloppy, and she often made careless arithmetic errors. When her papers were returned with red marks, she didn't seem to care; the math she learned at school wasn't nearly as interesting as the Sudoku puzzles she found in the newspaper. Ingrid got in trouble when her teacher saw the Stephen King novel she brought to school to read during free reading time. When Ingrid argued with the teacher about the meaning of free reading, she was sent to the office. The principal spoke to Ingrid before calling me to suggest a conference with the classroom teacher and school psychologist. At the conference, Ingrid's teacher expressed concerns about our daughter's attitude and her apparent lack of effort as evidenced by sloppy and incomplete worksheets, as well as inattentiveness in class. She was defensive when my husband and I expressed concerns about Ingrid's disinterest in school, the lack of challenging curriculum, and the amount of time spent on repetition. The teacher countered by describing Ingrid as an inattentive average student with few friends.

Discussion Questions

1. In what ways did Ingrid's behaviors differ from those of most infants, toddlers, and preschool children? Why was Ingrid's second-grade school experience so dramatically different from her first-grade experience?

2. What information, if any, should Ingrid's parents have shared with school personnel before she entered school? What information, if any, should the first-grade teacher have included in Ingrid's cumulative folder? Should teachers read student files before they meet new students or should they meet the student and then read the file? Why or why not?

3. In most school districts, identification of students for gifted services begins in second or third grade. What strategies can classroom teachers use to address the needs of students who exhibit gifted behaviors prior to program availability? What, if any, additional resources or support systems are needed?

4. In what ways can parents work with teachers to ensure that the needs of their children are met in a school setting? Whose responsibility is it to advocate for those needs? Why?

5. What role, if any, did birth order play in Ingrid's school experience?

Activities

1. What evidence-based practices in *Standard 4: Learning Environments* (see Appendix A) should be addressed when meeting the needs of Ingrid? Make a chart providing specific examples for the student outcomes and evidence-based practices.

2. Create a brochure for parents of preschool children in which you identify developmental milestones for children ages 2–5 years old.

3. Develop a lesson plan teaching letter sounds using tiered assignments for a mixed-ability classroom in which most students are learning letter sounds, a few know letter sounds and recognize sight words, and one is reading fluently.

4. Write a letter to the news outlet or parenting newsletter of your choice in which you offer tips for parents to talk to teachers when advocating for their child.

5. Produce an annotated bibliography of at least five books or articles on the characteristics and needs of young gifted learners. If possible, share with parents.

6. Construct a list of 10 ways in which parents and teachers of young children can collaborate to enhance student achievement and social and emotional growth.

Extensions

1. Create a variety of choice boards and task cards to be used to differentiate instruction in a subject of your choice and at the level of your choice.

2. Synthesize the research from at least three articles on the characteristics of profoundly gifted infants or preschool-age children. Present the information to your classmates or colleagues.

3. Working with a classmate or colleague, use a graphic organizer to represent 10 books for talented readers in primary grades. Identify the theme, genre, reading level, and plot for each selection.

4. Outline four topics of your choice to be used in a guided discussion group to increase social skills for second-grade students. Identify the goal, intended outcome, and activities for each discussion.

Additional Readings

Clark, B. (2012). *Growing up gifted: Developing the potential of children at school and at home* (8th ed.). Upper Saddle River, NJ: Pearson Education.

Colangelo, N., & Davis, G. A. (Eds.). (2002). *Handbook of gifted education* (3rd ed.). Boston, MA: Allyn & Bacon.

Coleman, L. J., & Cross, T. L. (2005). *Being gifted in school: An introduction to development, guidance, and teaching* (2nd ed.). Waco, TX: Prufrock Press.

Cross, T. L. (2004). *On the social and emotional lives of gifted children: Issues and factors in their psychological development* (4th ed.). Waco, TX: Prufrock Press.

Davis, G. A., Rimm, S. B., & Siegle, D. (2010). *Education of the gifted and talented* (6th ed.).Upper Saddle River, NJ: Pearson Education.

Delisle, J., & Galbraith, J. (2002). *When gifted kids don't have all the answers: How to meet their social and emotional needs*. Minneapolis, MN: Free Spirit.

Ferguson, S. K. (2009). Affective education: Addressing the social and emotional needs of gifted students in the classroom. In F. A. Karnes & S. M. Bean (Eds.), *Methods and materials for teaching the gifted* (3rd ed., pp. 447–482). Waco, TX: Prufrock Press.

Galbraith, J. (2009). *The gifted kids' survival guide: For ages 10 & under* (3rd ed.). Minneapolis, MN: Free Spirit.

Halsted, J. W. (2009). *Some of my best friends are books: Guiding gifted readers from preschool to high school* (3rd ed.). Scottsdale, AZ: Great Potential Press.

Porter, L. (2005). *Gifted young children: A guide for teachers and parents* (2nd ed.). New York, NY: Open University Press.

Rogers, K. B. (2002). *Re-forming gifted education: Matching the program to the child.* Scottsdale, AZ: Great Potential Press.

Whitney, C. S. (with Hirsch, G.). (2011). *Helping gifted children soar: A practical guide for parents and teachers* (2nd ed.). Scottsdale, AZ: Great Potential Press.

Chapter 6

⎯⎯⎯⎯◯⎯⎯⎯⎯

Providing a Continuum of Services

School districts should create a continuum of services for gifted students that are responsive to students' needs, talents, and abilities. The development of appropriate gifted education programming requires comprehensive services based on sound philosophical, theoretical, and empirical support. The following cases illustrate the challenges that are involved in providing appropriate educational services for gifted and talented students in a variety of settings.

Gifted Education Programming Standard 5: Programming

This standard encompasses programming options supporting comprehensive services that meet the cognitive, creative, and affective learning needs of the gifted and talented and the resources, policies, and procedures needed (see Appendix A).

Lenore School District

Introduction

More than 40% of all American schools are located in rural areas and 30% of all students in the United States attend rural schools (National Research Center on Rural Education Support [NRCRES], 2012). Rural districts typically serve small populations and have special challenges when planning to provide services for gifted and talented learners. Limited resources and access to trained staff and intellectual peers for gifted learners may be problematic in states where gifted and talented funding is based on student enrollment. These obstacles may be particularly challenging for rural districts that often are geographically isolated as well.

Low student enrollment may also permit greater flexibility for student placement and unique opportunities for acceleration of curriculum.

Lenore School District (LSD) is located in a rural community of 924 individuals, populated by generations of successful family farmers. During the previous school year, the district reported a K–12 student population of 696, of whom 1% were American Indian, 6% Latino, and 93% White. The school report card noted 4% of the students were English language learners (limited proficiency), 7% qualified for special education services, and 29% met the federal threshold for free and reduced lunch. High test scores, small classes, a 99% graduation rate, and a remarkably successful football team attracted 133 students from neighboring districts through open enrollment. Since 1924, one building, located in the center of town, has housed the K–12 student population and district offices.

Although Lenore does not have a formal gifted and talented program, upper elementary and secondary students have numerous opportunities to participate in afterschool enrichment activities. Last year, the district sent teams to academic competitions such as Math Masters, Knowledge Bowl, and Destination Imagination. The students had little success competing against larger school districts but enjoyed the experience. The annual science fair featured 17 student exhibits and attracted nearly the entire town.

Lenore is located in a state in which state statutes *permit* school districts and charter schools to identify and serve students who are gifted and talented, develop and evaluate programs, and provide staff development to ensure that students have access to challenging educational programs. Legislation also provides guidance for districts to adopt procedures for identifying gifted learners and *mandates* districts to adopt procedures for their academic acceleration. Categorical funding provided by the state for gifted and talented programs is $12 times the Adjusted Marginal Pupil Cost Unit (AMPCU), and expenditures are restricted to the following:

- identification of gifted and talented students,
- provision of education programs for gifted and talented students, and
- provision of staff development to prepare teachers to understand the unique instructional and affective needs of gifted and talented students.

Things to Consider

- *Gifted learners need instructional and socioemotional support systems.*
- *Rural districts are impacted by limited funding and limited access to supplemental learning resources that educators in cities and suburbs can easily access (Kordosky, 2011).*
- *Enrichment activities typically benefit all learners by providing an activity beyond the classroom curriculum to stimulate interest and excitement. This type of enrichment is provided for all students.*
- *According to Harry Passow (1996) and Karen Rogers (2002), what makes an activity particularly appropriate for a child with gifts or talents is when the following three questions are answered with "no":*
  - *Is this an activity that every child should be doing?*
  - *Is this an activity every child would like to do?*
  - *Is this an activity that every child is capable of doing?*

During the last school year, LSD received $9,652.00 for gifted and talented funding from the state. Some of the funds used supported the teams who participated in academic competition. The rest of the revenue went unspent and was recorded and carried over to the next fiscal year as required by state statute. The funds will remain restricted until spent for gifted and talented education at a later date. During the public comment portion of a recent school board meeting, a parent asked how the gifted and talented revenue has been spent and will be allocated for the next school year. She was surprised to learn the district did not spend the entire revenue, despite the lack of services for gifted and talented learners.

Discussion Questions

1. NAGC estimates that approximately 6% of children in the United States are gifted. Given its current enrollment, 42 of Lenore's K–12 students are

most likely gifted. Should the district broaden the definition of giftedness to identify and serve a larger percentage of the population? Support your rationale.

2. What is the best use of Lenore's gifted and talented revenue? Should the district dedicate its resources to programming that occurs within the school day or largely based on afterschool enrichment? Support your rationale.

3. How should the Lenore School District plan to meet the needs of gifted and talented learners? Should all revenue spent be within a fiscal year or are there circumstances in which it is advantageous to carry some funds into the next? Support your rationale.

4. What special challenges and opportunities for meeting the needs of gifted and talented learners occur in small school districts?

Activities

1. Lenore School District exists in a local control state. The law permits, but does not require, districts to identify and serve gifted and talented learners. Identification and service models vary greatly throughout the state. Create a plan for the first meeting of Lenore School District's newly created Gifted and Talented Task Force. What should be the task force's first steps?

2. *Standard 5.1 Variety of Programming* (see Appendix A) references a variety of programming for gifted learners. What are the attributes of high-quality, evidenced-based programming for gifted learners in small school districts? Devise an outline for comprehensive services for Lenore's gifted and talented population.

3. Prepare a compelling presentation to the Lenore School Board justifying the creation of a gifted and talented program and the allocation of resources that may possibly exceed funding provided by the state.

4. Identify six different distance learning opportunities to use that may augment local resources and accelerate K–12 instruction. Create educator guidelines for the use of distance learning within and outside of the school day.

Extensions

1. Review *Standard 6: Professional Development* (see Appendix A) and create a professional development plan for the Lenore school staff. Consider the following:
   - Who should receive training on the nature and needs of gifted learners?

- How should the training be delivered?
- How might the use of technology help archive materials for future use?

2. Create an agenda for a presentation to an Advisory Committee in which you will explain how and why a task force has formed. Identify resources that you think will be appropriate for the parents.
3. Research the 2007 Javits Grant, Project Rural Education Accelerated Learning (REAL), and its impact on schools and families in rural Pennsylvania. In what ways did the collaboration of the regional service center and the state build capacity to serve gifted learners? Write a similar 250-word abstract for a grant proposal to replicate Project REAL in your state.
4. Create an annotated bibliography of 12 gifted and talented resources for a school professional development library.

Additional Readings

Benjamin, A. (2005). *Differentiated instruction using technology: A guide for middle and high school teachers.* Larchmont, NY: Eye on Education.

Delisle, J., & Galbraith, J. (2002). *When gifted kids don't have all the answers: How to meet their social and emotional needs.* Minneapolis, MN: Free Spirit.

Heacox, D. (2009). *Making differentiation a habit: How to ensure success in academically diverse classrooms.* Minneapolis, MN: Free Spirit.

Howley, A., Rhodes, M., & Beall, J. (2009). Challenges facing rural schools: Implications for gifted students. *Journal for the Education of the Gifted, 32,* 515–536.

Leavitt, M. (2007). *Building a gifted program: Identifying and educating gifted students in your school.* Scottsdale, AZ: Great Potential Press.

Purcell, J., & Eckert, R. (Eds.). (2006). *Designing services and programs for high-ability learners: A guidebook for gifted education.* Thousand Oaks, CA: Corwin Press.

Martin

Introduction

The publication of A Nation Deceived: How Schools Hold Back America's Brightest Students *by Nicholas Colangelo, Susan G. Assouline, and Miraca U. M. Gross (2004) documents the benefits of acceleration on the academic growth and socioemotional development of gifted and talented learners. Since its publication, many states in the United States have enacted legislation that either supports or requires academic acceleration.*

This case study introduces the education professional to Martin, a second-grade student residing in a state requiring the academic acceleration of gifted and talented learners.

The Washington Elementary School gifted and talented coordinator contacted the state gifted and talented education specialist to request a phone conference and assistance with a delicate situation. The education specialist was invited by the coordinator to attend a child study team meeting to discuss the possibility of grade acceleration for a second-grade student. The coordinator expressed concern that the proposed acceleration would not be in the best interest of the student and hoped to clarify her understanding of the state acceleration mandate.

During the phone conference, the coordinator conveyed the following: A parent had contacted her son's second-grade teacher early in the school year, to request her son's acceleration into a third-grade classroom. The parent assured the teacher that her son, Martin, liked his classroom teacher very much but admitted that he was bored with second-grade work. After expressing his surprise, the teacher referred the parent to the district's website where she was able to print a copy of the district's acceleration procedure and the protocol for requesting a special needs assessment. That evening, Martin's mother completed the required forms and gave them to her son to return to his teacher the next morning.

During his preparation period, the teacher delivered the paperwork to the secretary, who notified the child study team. Following district protocol, the secretary scheduled the meeting and e-mailed the required notices to the team. Purposely for the meeting, she notified the building principal, school psychologist, gifted and talented coordinator, a Title I teacher, as well as Martin's first- and second-grade teachers.

Martin's Mother

Martin's mother is confident that the team will honor her request; after all, Martin is smart, mature, and nearly a head taller than his classmates. He will soon turn 8 and she wants to be able to invite all of the third-grade boys to his birthday party. Martin's mother heard from a neighbor that, as required by law, the district must accelerate gifted and talented students. She researched the state statute and found the mandate on the State Department of Education's website. She read the summary and learned that districts are required to "adopt procedures for the academic acceleration of gifted and talented students that includes an assessment of students' readiness and motivation for acceleration and a match between the curriculum and the students' academic needs." In her mind, Martin is ready, motivated, and capable of third-grade work. More importantly, Martin is the same age as the majority of students in third grade.

Things to Consider

- *Acceleration is an academic intervention that moves students through an educational program at a rate faster or an age younger than what is typical.*
- *Acceleration requires high academic ability and helps match the level, complexity, and pace of the curriculum with the readiness and motivation of the student.*
- *The decision to accelerate a child should be made after careful consideration of the student's instructional and socioemotional needs and other pertinent information.*
- *The publication* A Nation Deceived *(Colangelo et al., 2004) identified 18 different forms of acceleration, many of which can be managed by well-trained education professionals within the regular classroom.*

The Teacher

Following protocol, each member of the child study team prepared for the meeting by gathering relevant materials. Martin's second-grade teacher reviewed the cumulative file, which included the Kindergarten Readiness Assessment, report cards, state tests scores, samples of classroom work, and comments written by his former teachers. The teacher confirmed that Martin's performance has been consistently average to high average in all areas. He read the first-grade teacher's end-of-year comments, describing Martin as a happy, well-adjusted student. The records provided no evidence of classroom work, abilities, or maturity that differed markedly than that expected of a first-grade student.

After collecting several samples of Martin's second-grade work, the teacher contacted the gifted and talented coordinator. He explained that he found no evidence that Martin is a gifted learner and confessed his surprise toward the request for grade level acceleration. Because Martin has not qualified for services, the coordinator has no personal knowledge of the student. She asked the teacher a number of questions and then carefully examined the file. She noted no salience other than Martin's age. Martin is at least a year older than his classmates.

The Team

The child study team meeting began with a review of the parent's written rationale for the request. Martin's mother noted that her son is physically and emotionally mature. She described him as a smart boy, easily bored, and in need of a better match between the curriculum and his academic needs. She cited the state statute mandating acceleration and added that Martin should be accelerated to the level of his peers.

The Decision

The team reviewed the protocol and files before coming to a consensus that there is no evidence to support acceleration at this time. They recommended the classroom teacher monitor Martin more closely and offer additional opportunities for differentiated instruction. The next morning, the psychologist completed the report and phoned Martin's mother to notify her of the team's decision. Martin's mother expressed her disappointment and revealed she delayed her son's entrance into kindergarten in an effort to ensure better behavior and better grades. The conversation ended abruptly. Martin's mother vowed to take the issue to the superintendent to ensure her son's right to acceleration was not violated.

Discussion Questions

1. Is the state acceleration mandate relevant to Martin's case? Why or why not?
2. In what ways does Martin differ from the students in his second-grade class? From the students in the third-grade class? Is the degree of difference enough to warrant assessment for giftedness?
3. *Standard 5: Programming* (see Appendix A) references a variety of programming in which students with gifts and talents participate in evidenced-based programming options that enhance performance in cognitive and affective areas. Would Martin benefit from additional program

opportunities, such as multiple forms of grouping, enrichment, resource rooms, or special classes?

4. Should the team accelerate Martin if his abilities and performance are in the average- to high-average range? Is it in Martin's best interest for the team to consider him for whole-grade acceleration?

5. Did the team make the right decision? Why or why not?

Activities

1. With your colleagues, conduct a mock child study team meeting to consider Martin's needs.

2. Plan a conference with Martin and his parents in which you discuss the proposed acceleration and the team's decision. What information will you share? What evidenced-based information can you provide to support the decision?

3. *Evidence-Based Practices 5.6 Policies and Procedures* (see Appendix A) recognizes the need for students with gifts and talents to participate in regular and gifted education programs that are guided by clear policies and procedures that provide for advanced learning needs. Create a list of policies and procedures to guide and sustain two of the following components of your district's or campus' gifted and talented program: assessment, identification, acceleration practices, or grouping practices built on an evidence-based foundation in gifted education.

Extensions

1. Locate and research two states with acceleration mandates. How do they differ from each other? What are the strengths and weaknesses of the mandates?

2. Write a 500-word letter to the editor identifying challenges and possible solutions for whole-grade or subject acceleration of elementary students.

3. Design and articulate a plan to conduct a longitudinal study on the effect of whole-grade acceleration on elementary students in your district. Include the following in your plan: acceleration tool or protocol, system for data collection, sample size, and timeline.

Additional Readings

Assouline, S., Colangelo, N., Lupkowski-Shoplik, A., Lipscomb, J., & Forstadt, L. (2009). *Iowa Acceleration Scale, manual: A guide for whole-grade acceleration K–8* (3rd ed.). Scottsdale, AZ: Great Potential Press.

Institute for Research on Acceleration Policy, National Association for Gifted Children, & Council of State Directors of Programs for the Gifted. (2009). *Guidelines for developing an academic acceleration policy.* Iowa City, IA: Authors. Retrieved from http://www.accelerationinstitute.org

National Association for Gifted Children, & Council of State Directors for Programs for the Gifted (2010–2011). *State of the nation in gifted education.* Washington, DC: Author. Retrieved from http://www.nagc.org/uploaded-Files/Information_and_Resources/2010-11_state_of_states/State%20of%20 the%20Nation%20%20(final).pdf

Plucker, J. A., & Callahan, C. M. (Eds.). (2008). *Critical issues and practices in gifted education: What the research says* (1st ed.). Waco, TX: Prufrock Press.

Roberts, J. L. (2005). *Enrichment opportunities for gifted learners.* Waco, TX: Prufrock Press.

Smutny, J. F., Walker, S. Y., & Meckstroth, E. A. (2007). *Acceleration for gifted learners, K–5.* Thousand Oaks, CA: Corwin Press.

VanTassel-Baska, J. (2005). *Acceleration strategies for teaching gifted learners.* Waco, TX: Prufrock Press.

Skylar School District

Introduction

Developing a strong, defensible program for the education of gifted and talented learners requires careful planning and periodic evaluation. High quality programs are comprehensive, coordinated and seek equity and excellence. They adhere to best practices and national standards.

This case study introduces the education professional to a school district located in a state where identification and programs for gifted and talented learners are mandated but not monitored. In this state, districts are required to submit a plan to the state department of instruction for gifted education programs every 3 years.

Skylar School District (SSD) is located in a community of 14,500. The hardwood forests, recreational activities, and proximity to beautiful lakes are what make the community known. The population is stable, with its local economy driven by tourism and a healthy lumber industry. Over the years, visitors enamored with the scenic vistas and available waterfront property have built homes along the lake's shores. Modest family vacation cabins, which once lined the shores, have been replaced by full-service resorts and imposing mansions with their private docks and boathouses. Local coffee shops have given way to big box retailers and restaurants.

During the last year, SSD reported a K–12 student population of 6,665 of whom 92% are White, 1% American Indian, 1% Black, and 6% Hispanic. The school report noted that 18% of the students qualified for special education services, 3% were English language learners, and 38% met federal guidelines for free and reduced lunch. There are five elementary schools, two middle schools, a high school, and an alternative high school. The district reported a 94% graduation rate.

In Skylar, acceleration of instruction occurs through program placement and within the regular classroom. District personnel have resisted subject and whole-grade acceleration. Board policy has prohibited early admission to kindergarten. All school enrichment occurs during school hours and through a variety of after-school opportunities.

The district employs a gifted and talented education program coordinator and one gifted education specialist. The coordinator provides curriculum extensions and differentiated instruction coaching to K–8 staff upon request. Each spring, the coordinator is responsible for the identification of gifted learners for placement in Lakes Elementary, the full-time program for highly gifted learners, and for placement of students in cluster classrooms at other schools within the district. State test scores in mathematics and reading as well as teacher recommendations determine the pool of candidates. Each pool candidate is administered the Wechsler Intelligence Scale for Children®—Fourth Edition (WISC- IV). Parents are not included in the process but may request an assessment.

The gifted education specialist spends one day each week staffing a resource room at each of the four remaining elementary schools. Students identified as gifted are able to visit the resource room for 50 minutes each week. During their time in the resource room, these students work on special projects and interact with others of similar interests and abilities. Most students in the pull-out program enjoy the opportunity to visit the resource room, especially when they are not required to make up their regular classroom work. On Fridays, the specialist works with teams preparing for academic competition. The specialist also maintains the district's gifted and talented webpage with a list of afterschool enrichment opportunities, competition results, and links to relevant state and national gifted organizations.

Things to consider

- *Gifted learners exist in every population.*
- *The demographics of the participants in a district gifted and talented program should closely mirror the demographics of the entire district.*
- *High-quality programs have transparent identification procedures.*
- *High-quality programs use research-based assessment practices and offer an array of services to address cognitive and affective needs.*
- *High-quality programs have an evaluation cycle.*

According to the district's website, students must achieve a minimum score of 95% on state assessments and achieve 130 or above on the WISC-IV to receive placement at Lakes Elementary. Over the years, Lakes Elementary has earned a reputation as a school for students whose families are wealthy and capable of providing their children with unlimited support and enrichment opportunities.

Students are clustered in heterogeneous classrooms based on high scores of 95% or above on state tests, but less than 130 on the WISC-IV. The pull-out program serves students who score 90% or above on state reading or math assessments, but do not qualify for either Lakes Elementary or the district's cluster classrooms.

A recent review of the district demographics from data reported to the state has revealed that Lakes Elementary School's full-time gifted program comprises a 2% free and reduced lunch population and no students of color.

A local parent group has initiated discussions about what appears to be discrepancies between the district's criteria for placement at Lakes Elementary and the school's actual population. Concerned for student equity and a possible opportunity gap, the parents have requested a review of gifted services identification and placement procedures. They question the district's reliance on achievement as the primary indicator of general intelligence.

Discussion Questions

1. Is the Skylar School District's system of student identification and placement consistent with best practices in the field of gifted education? What might account for the absence of gifted students with low socioeconomic status or gifted students of color at Lakes Elementary? Is a further investigation warranted? Why or why not?

2. Does inclusion of diverse students require different tools for assessment? What would be the methodology to use in order to more efficiently and equitably identify students for gifted and talented services?

3. Which of the six NAGC Pre-K–Grade 12 Programming Standards (see Appendix A) will inform the process requested by Skylar parents (e.g., learning and development, assessment, curriculum planning and instruction, learning environments, programming, professional development)? Does one standard take priority? Why?

4. What model of service best describes the district's current gifted and talented education program? Are the services comprehensive? Why or why not?

5. What best practices support defensible programs for the gifted? Does Skylar School District have a defensible program for gifted learners? Why or why not?

Activities

1. Create a plan and timeline for evaluation of the district's services. The plan should identify the necessary data for collection and review, participant roles and assignment of responsibilities.

2. Prepare a research-based presentation for the Skylar School Board, defending the current program model chosen by the district to serve gifted and talented learners.

3. Develop a compelling research-based presentation for the Skylar School Board, which supports a foundation recommending a new service model.

4. Review with a partner *Standard 5: Programming* related to the *Evidence-Based Practices* (see Appendix A) of critical components providing a systematic and continuous delivery of service (Johnsen, 2012). Which components are missing from the Skylar School District service model? In what ways can we enhance the current level of services? Create a list.
   - comprehensive and coordinated services (5.2 and 5.5),
   - collaboration in schools and with families (5.3),
   - career and talent development pathways (5.7),
   - policies and procedures (5.6), and
   - resources (5.4)

Extensions

1. Create a PowerPoint presentation on the benefits of full-time gifted programs for elementary aged students. The PowerPoint should highlight scientifically based practices and outline the process and timeline for student application.
2. What credentials, training, and experience are desirable for classroom teachers, counselors, and administrators assigned to full-time gifted programs? What interview questions would you ask of perspective teachers, counselors, and administrators? Make a list.
3. Create an identification matrix that is sensitive to traditionally underrepresented populations and grounded in best practices. Include a timeline and process for evaluation.

Additional Readings

Callahan, C. M. (2004). *Program evaluation in gifted education..* Thousand Oaks, CA: Corwin Press.

Ford, D. Y. (2004). *Intelligence testing and cultural diversity: Concerns, cautions and considerations*. Storrs: University of Connecticut, The National Research Center on the Gifted and Talented. Retrieved from http://www.gifted.uconn.edu/nrcgt/ford5.html

Johnsen, S. K. (2004). Making decisions about placement. In S.K. Johnsen (Ed.), *Identifying gifted students: A practical guide* (pp. 107–131). Waco, TX: Prufrock Press.

Johnsen, S. K. (2005). *Identifying gifted students: A step-by-step guide*. Waco, TX: Prufrock Press.

Leavitt, M. (2007). *Building a gifted program: Identifying and educating gifted students in your school*. Scottsdale, AZ: Great Potential Press.

Purcell, J., & Eckert, R. (Eds.). (2006). *Designing services and programs for high-ability learners: A guidebook for gifted education.* Thousand Oaks, CA: Corwin Press.

Rogers, K. B. (2002). *Re-forming gifted education: Matching the program to the child.* Scottsdale, AZ: Great Potential Press.

Slocumb, P. D., & Payne, R. K. (2000). *Removing the mask: Giftedness in poverty.* Highlands, TX: Aha! Process.

VanTassel-Baska, J. L. (Ed.). (2007). *Serving gifted learners beyond the traditional classroom: A guide to alternative programs and services* Waco, TX: Prufrock Press.

VanTassel-Baska, J. L. (Ed.). (2008). *Alternative assessments with gifted and talented students.* Waco, TX: Prufrock Press.

STARS

Introduction

Many school districts offer sound program services for gifted and talented children in the elementary grades and rely on advanced courses for students in grades 6–12. The transition years, grades 6–8, are often years of frustration for parents of the gifted and talented, who strive to keep the intellectual fires burning within their children, and for the children, who strive to maintain their curiosity about the world around them. The structure of some middle years' programs prevents acceleration and enrichment for gifted and talented learners. This case looks at one school's effort to provide both intellectual engagement, as well as course acceleration, for gifted and talented students in the middle years. The case presents dilemmas that many schools face when developing new program services.

The development and implementation of STARS (Securing Talent: Acceleration and Rigor for Success) is presented in this case to highlight the use of the NAGC Pre-K–Grade 12 Gifted Programming Standard 5: Programming *(see Appendix A) for schools that struggle with middle years' programs for gifted and talented.*

Warm Springs Independent School District

Warm Springs Independent School District (WSISD) is a small urban district that serves 15,000 students in prekindergarten through grade 12. There are 15 elementary schools, six middle schools, and two high schools. The 15 elementary schools offer weekly pull-out services for their gifted and talented students. Their elementary school classroom teachers are encouraged to preassess the students to determine acceleration needs. The teachers of the pull-out classes offer differentiated instructional strategies for general education classroom teachers.

Due to parental concerns, WSISD is faced with providing services that are more appropriate for gifted and talented students in sixth through eighth grade. Many parents have moved their students from the public middle schools to smaller districts surrounding the WSISD, or into one of a variety of private school offerings. Parents have indicated that their children will remain if the district is able to meet their expectations for gifted and talented services.

> ## Things to Consider
>
> - *Parents want the optimal services for their gifted and talented children. Educators want to include research-based best practices when designing and implementing curriculum and instruction for gifted and talented learners. These two points of view must be reconciled for the best possible services.*
> - *The Pre-K–Grade 12 NAGC Gifted Programming Standards provide an excellent guide for developing gifted and talented services (see Appendix A). How they align with local standards and parental expectations will determine the success of any new program service.*

The Challenge

WSISD has taken its lead for considering and making program changes from the *NAGC Pre-K–Grade 12 Gifted Education Programming Standards* (2010; see Appendix A). District educators embarked on a book study of *NAGC Pre-K–Grade 12 Gifted Education Programming Standards: A Guide to Planning and Implementing High-Quality Services* (Johnsen, 2012). After a six-week book study, WSISD educators' focus is on the work's five critical components for a quality program that offers a continuum of services; below are the components that reflect the NAGC standards (Johnsen, 2012):

- comprehensive and coordinated services (5.5 and 5.2),
- collaboration in schools and with families (5.3),
- career and talent development pathways (5.7),
- policies and procedures (5.6), and
- resources (5.4). (p. 153)

In addition to the program services, WSISD uses the NAGC Pre-K–Grade 12 Gifted Programming Standards for alternatives to meet students' cognitive and affective areas. *Evidence-Based Practices 5.1.1* through *5.1.5* remind educators that evidence-based options should include acceleration and enrichment both during school hours and outside the school, as well as multiple grouping arrangements, mentorships, internships, virtual schools, and all types of assistive technologies (see Appendix A).

WSISD has opted to redesign middle school services that include the research-based best practices listed previously. They are determined to make sure that the infusion of career pathways and technology occurs in all content areas. They also want to make certain that along with their services for gifted and talented learners, general education and special education are part of any plan formerly developed. In order to make this happen, school counselors, school psychologists, social workers, and other constituents participate in the planning.

Their first step is to focus on administrative support. Support needs to include all central office administrators and the local board of education. The request of monetary resources is necessary to support curriculum, field experiences, technology, and course acceleration needs. Autonomy is also required in order to select teachers and campus leaders for STARS.

Their second step is to design services that will follow the best practices. Then, they will present these services to administrators, parents, interested students, and the community. After creating the design for STARS, the educators responsible for the implementation of the design can develop procedures and policies to guide other educators, parents, and students.

An innovative plan for a WSISD middle school is underway.

Discussion Questions

1. What are the most pressing issues to consider when developing a program for middle school students? Why? In what ways do these needs differ from the development of elementary school program?
2. What dilemmas will educators working together face in the development of STARS? How could they be overcome?
3. Why does a "one-size-fits-all" philosophy, in terms of design and implementation of a program, not work for meeting the needs of all students?
4. In what ways should students, parents, and other constituents have input into the design of the STARS program?
5. When planning the design, in what ways can STARS implement acceleration and enrichment?
6. What is effective differentiation? What special challenges do secondary teachers face when differentiating curriculum within their classrooms?
7. Would the integration of content across subjects be appropriate for STARS? Would integration facilitate or interfere with students' acceleration and enrichment? Why or why not?
8. What policies and procedures must one consider when developing any program for gifted learners?

Activities

1. One idea the educators have for STARS is minicourses in which students research areas of interest that may lead to presentations of their learning and career explorations. Determine an area of interest (e.g., robotics or

cartooning), and develop an outline of a minicourse for middle school students. Identify possible resources for the minicourse.

2. Design a classroom that would facilitate classroom management for differentiated learning. Consider including student interest centers, learning stations, research centers, technology stations, and any ideas you have in terms of a floor plan for your STARS classroom. Label each area and include a brief description of how students will utilize each area.

3. Research virtual school options for gifted and talented students in grades 6–8. Create a compendium of options.

4. How would you staff a STARS middle school with 300 students in grades 6, 7, and 8? Create a staffing pattern that meets state requirements and includes personnel requirements and design.

5. What resources would be most helpful in the planning of a new program for the gifted? Develop an annotated list to share.

Extensions

1. Using an online tool, create a needs assessment for parents, teachers, and/or administrators to determine what programming areas and services are essential in a district.

2. Using *Evidence-Based Practices 5.5.1* (see Appendix A), create a chart that indicates the stages of implementation for a multiyear program that includes grades 6–8 and 9–12.

3. Develop a sample curriculum policy for a magnet program in your district.

4. Develop a budget that would support the start-up of a magnet program. Include line items for staffing, professional development, curriculum purchases, and other resources in your budget.

5. Using a graphic organizer, prepare a presentation for the board of education that compares and contrasts two models of programs and services for gifted learners. Be prepared to answer questions about the programs, such as which ones are more effective and why. Suggest a recommendation for the adaptation of a particular program.

Additional Readings

Brighton, K. (2007). *Coming of age: The education and development of young adolescents.* Westerville, OH: National Middle School Association.

Burns, J., Jenkins, J. B., & Kane, J. T. (2011). *Advisory: Finding the best fit for your school.* Westerville, OH: Association for Middle Level Education.

Delisle, J., & Galbraith, J. (2002). *When gifted kids don't have all the answers: How to meet their social and emotional needs.* Minneapolis, MN: Free Spirit.

Galbraith, J., & Delisle, J. (2011). *The gifted teen survival guide: Smart, sharp, and ready for (almost) anything* (4th ed.). Minneapolis, MN: Free Spirit.

Kaplan, S., & Cannon, M. W. (2001). *Lessons from the middle: High-end learning for middle school students.* Waco, TX: Prufrock Press.

Kolodziej, N. (2010). *Learning station models for middle grades.* Westerville, OH: National Middle School Association.

National Association for Gifted Children. (n.d.). *Meeting the needs of high ability and high potential learners in the middle grades* [Position statement]. Retrieved from http://www.nagc.org/index.aspx?id=400

Rakow, S. (2011). *Educating gifted students in middle school: A practical guide* (2nd ed.). Waco, TX: Prufrock Press.

Schurr, S. (2012). *Authentic assessment: Active, engaging product and performance measures.* Westerville, OH: Association for Middle Level Education.

Silver, D. (2012). *Fall down 7 times, get up 8: Teaching kids to succeed.* Thousand Oaks, CA: Corwin Press.

Stockton, C. (2011). *Minds and motion: Active learning for the creative classroom.* Westerville, OH: National Middle School Association.

Strahan, D. B., L'Esperance, M., & Van Hoose, J. (2009). *Promoting harmony: Young adolescent development and classroom practices* (3rd ed.). Westerville, OH: National Middle School Association.

Tomlinson, C. A. (1995). *Gifted learners and the middle school: Problem or promise?* [ERIC EC Digest E535]. Retrieved from http://www.nagc.org/index.aspx?id=150

Tomlinson, C. A., & Doubet, K. (2006). *Smart in the middle grades: Classrooms that work for bright middle schoolers.* Westerville, OH: National Middle School Association.

Tomlinson, C. A., & Imbeau, M. B. (2010). *Leading and managing a differentiated classroom.* Alexandria, VA: ASCD.

Tomlinson, C. A., & Imbeau, M. B. (2011). *Managing a differentiated classroom, grades K–8: A practical guide.* New York, NY: Scholastic.

Tomlinson, C. A., & McTighe, J. (2006). *Integrating differentiated instruction and understanding by design: Connecting content and kids.* Alexandria, VA: ASCD.

Avery, Ethan, and Brazos

Introduction

Identification of very young gifted students is rare, and curriculum accommodations for them are often scarce. This case centers on the identification of and appropriate setting for three young, highly gifted children. This case describes three very gifted, yet very diverse primary-age children. Although their abilities and needs are different, there are commonalities that can be accommodated through like settings and parallel curriculum opportunities.

Avery, Ethan, and Brazos

Avery is 3 years old. She has come to this school because they will accept her into kindergarten as a 3-year-old. Avery spoke her first words at 9 months when she read the name of the cereal from the box. By 18 months, she had appeared on a national television show displaying her reading from a book and answering questions about what she read.

Avery's parents relate that she plays for hours with Veement, her imaginary friend. They play games that she invents. If Avery does not want to play with Veement, she says that his mom came by to take him home.

In addition to nurturing her reading and comprehension abilities, the school works with Avery on her gross and fine motor skills, which are typical for a 3-year-old. Her teacher gives her manipulatives to work with numbers because she is average for a 5-year-old in math. Although she can memorize quite well, she prefers to know why and how, rather than just give back information.

One of her new friends in kindergarten is Ethan, who is 5. Ethan likes many of the things Avery does, but sometimes complains that she is too bossy. Ethan also excels beyond his age mates in several areas. He has a mature sense of humor and likes joke books. He enjoys trying his jokes on the other children even if they don't understand them. Only Avery and his teacher "get" them. His teacher has introduced Ethan and Avery to puns. Ethan told Ms. Bowden that he likes them; they are *punny*.

Ethan is also interested in science and math. These subjects fascinate him as much as reading and storytelling do Avery. Although Avery likes fairy tales and making up her own books, Ethan wants to read only nonfiction books that tell him how things work. Avery has a collection of fictional stories about girls who get into mischief. Ethan has a collection of rocks that he has labeled and, with his mom's help, mounted for a display like the ones in the museums.

Another student in the class is Brazos. Brazos walked at the age of one and talked in complete sentences by the age of 2. Brazos is extremely introverted. He rarely talks to anyone, but when he does, it is to talk about his feelings or to ask questions about things he has seen or something he has heard. He is sensitive to issues related to justice and fairness. He does not understand why some children bully or hit others. He is also very sensitive to tags in his clothes.

Brazos can concentrate for long periods of time, especially when he works on difficult puzzles. If he is in the "Brazos zone", he may have to be physically touched to get his attention. Sometimes the teacher watches him as he sits and stares into space. If she asks him what he is thinking, he may say, "Just something," or he may start to tell her a long, imaginative story.

Things to Consider

- *Young, highly gifted children display a variety of characteristics.*
- *Parents of young gifted children may or may not realize their child is different from age mates.*
- *Specialized curriculum and appropriate settings are essential for young gifted learners' academic and social growth.*

The Kindergarten Teacher

The kindergarten teacher has never had experiences like this before. She sees Avery for the prodigy she is and welcomes the challenge Avery brings. Even though Avery is beyond her age peers in many areas, Ms. Bowden also recognizes Avery's limitations as a 3-year-old. She knows that she must balance Avery's academic abilities with her physical and emotional needs.

Although Ms. Bowden knew that she would have Avery as a part of her class, she didn't expect two other students to arrive with similar yet differing needs and abilities. Within a few days of school, she realized the challenges these three students bring to her class. Aligning her teaching strategies to support the learning and developmental differences among gifted preschool-age children is but one of the challenges she faces. Her balancing act of meeting the needs of Avery, Brazos, and Ethan, along with 18 other students in her class, will make for an interesting and enlightening year.

Discussion Questions

1. Do you think each of these students is gifted, or have adults nurtured them to exhibit gifted behaviors? Support your beliefs.
2. Is it appropriate to place a 3-year-old in a kindergarten classroom? If not, what other arrangements could be made for Avery in a public school?
3. How does Brazos' extreme introversion affect classroom activities? In what ways will his curriculum be differentiated to accommodate his needs? Should he be evaluated to determine if he falls into the autism spectrum?
4. What other campus resources could Ms. Bowden use to help her work with these three students, as well as the 18 others?
5. Discuss asynchronous development and how it affects the decisions Mrs. Bowden should make related to meeting the needs of Avery, Brazos, and Ethan.
6. What type of support do these gifted children need for their social growth? How might their social needs change as they go through the elementary grades?

Activities

1. This scenario does not include a parent's perspective. Write a brief scenario from the view of the parents of Avery, Brazos, or Ethan from personal experience and/or using the Additional Readings.
2. Create a physical diagram of Ms. Bowden's classroom that illustrates how she accommodates all of her students, including Avery, Brazos, and Ethan.
3. Define the characteristics of each of the three students using a Venn diagram or graphic organizer of your choice to compare and contrast their characteristics. Create a center activity based on their common characteristics. (*Note:* Additional Readings will facilitate this activity.)
4. Create a crossword puzzle that includes characteristics of young gifted children. Use this activity in a professional development session that you present to teachers of primary-age students.
5. View the movie *The Incredibles* or *Akeelah and the Bee*. Compare and contrast the character(s) in the movie you select to Avery, Ethan, and/or Brazos through a poem, a short story, or a picture book. (*Note:* http://www.hoagiesgifted.org/movies provides an extensive list of movies for or about gifted children and young adults.)

Extensions

1. Create a unit of study for a young gifted child in your classroom or on your campus.
2. Write an article for a professional journal describing a young gifted child you know or have taught and the challenges and rewards in teaching the student.
3. Research a variety of school districts and/or states that have options for very young gifted children. Develop a compendium of your findings.
4. Create a kindergarten through fifth grade curriculum timeline for one of the students.
5. From the timeline in #4, describe options for the students in grades 6–12.
6. Are there unique issues involved when meeting the needs of young gifted children? Why or why not? Develop an annotated bibliography of resources for parents and/or teachers related to this topic.

Additional Readings

Daniels, S., & Piechowski, M. M. (Eds.). (2009). *Living with intensity: Understanding the sensitivity, excitability, and emotional development of gifted children, adolescents, and adults.* Scottsdale, AZ: Great Potential Press.

Morelock, M. J., & Feldman, D. H. (1992). The assessment of giftedness in preschool children. In E. V. Nuttall, I. Romero, & J. Kalesnik (Eds.), *Assessing and screening preschoolers: Psychological and educational dimensions* (pp. 301–309). Boston, MA: Allyn & Bacon.

Olszewski-Kubilius, P., Limburg-Weber, L., & Pfeiffer, S. (2003). *Early gifts: Recognizing and nurturing children's talents.* Waco, TX: Prufrock Press.

Porter, L. (2005). *Gifted young children: A guide for teachers and parents* (2nd ed.). New York, NY: Open University Press.

Robinson, N. M., & Weimer, L. J. (1991). Selection of candidates for early admission to and first grade. In W. T. Southern & E. D. Jones (Eds.), *The academic acceleration of gifted children* (pp. 29–50). New York, NY: Teachers College Press. Retrieved from http://www.davidsongifted.org/db/Articles_id_10123.aspx

Saunders, J., & Espeland, P. (1991). B*ringing out the best: A guide for parents of young gifted children* (Rev. ed.). Minneapolis, MN: Free Spirit.

Shaklee, B. (2005, May). *Young gifted children.* SENG Update. Retrieved from http://www.sengifted.org/archives/articles/young-gifted-children

Smutny, J. F., & von Fremd, S. E. (2004*). Differentiating for the young child: Teaching strategies across the content areas, K–3.* Thousand Oaks, CA: Corwin Press.

Tolan, S. S. (1992). Parents vs. theorists: Dealing with the exceptionally gifted. *Roeper Review, 15*(1), 14–18. doi:10.1080/02783199209553450

Verdick, E., & Reeve, E. (2012). *The survival guide for kids with autism spectrum disorders: And their parents.* Minneapolis, MN: Free Spirit.

Webb, J. T., Amend, E. R., Webb, N. E., Goerss, J., Beljan, P., & Olenchak, F. R. (2005). *Misdiagnosis and dual diagnosing of gifted children and adults: ADHD, Bipolar, OCD, Asperger's, Depression, and other disorders.* Scottsdale, AZ: Great Potential Press.

Chapter 7

Planning for Professional Development

Educators, along with parents, play a key role in helping a gifted and talented student reach his or her full potential. Understanding the social-emotional and cognitive needs of gifted students requires that all educators involved in the development and implementation of gifted programs be involved in professional development. Professional development can be provided in many ways and should be a key component of any defensible program for gifted students. Professional expertise is guided by standards in the field, which include the NAGC-CEC-TAG (2006) Teacher Standards for Gifted and Talented Education and the National Staff Development Standards available from http://www.ncate.org/LinkClick. aspx?fileticket=5zapZLBPUhQ%3D&tabid=676). The following cases explore the need for different types of professional development opportunities and the ways they may be offered.

Gifted Education Programming Standard 6: Professional Development

This standard refers to building knowledge and skills with administrators, teachers, counselors, and other instructional support staff (see Appendix A).

Rosamaria

Introduction

ESL/ELL students' learning strengths are often overlooked. Barriers such as communication with parents and lack of understanding of cultural differences by educators who make service decisions create hesitancy for school personnel to pursue gifted services for this population of students.

Rosamaria's case study addresses the need for professional development to help school districts deal with the dilemma of balancing learning needs and strengths for students from backgrounds different than majority students.

This case also includes the impact of Response to Intervention (RtI) on all students, including those from different cultures.

Rosamaria

Rosamaria is 12 years old and in the sixth grade. Even though she was born in the United States, her parents are immigrants from Mexico. Her parents, Jose and Elsa, are able to converse in English, but Spanish is their primary language at home. Even though they were able to stay in the United States with a green card for many years, they recently received their citizenship papers. Now everyone in the family is a citizen of the U.S. Rosamaria's father works at a local plant in the Southeast that makes parts for refrigerators and her mother works part-time in a flower shop just down the street from the school. They live in a house that they are currently renting.

Rosamaria has a younger sister, Yolanda, and a younger brother, Juan Jose. All three children are in school and all three make the honor roll each 6 weeks. Their parents attend school functions when their jobs allow them to do so or teacher conferences when requested by the teacher or principal.

Rosamaria's teachers have always commented on how bright she is in the classroom. She learned English very quickly when she started in school and she liked making up rhymes with her new language. Rosamaria is very good at math and asks many questions when studying science, especially in lab work. When her class is studying history, she makes connections to the stories of Mexico and its history that her parents tell her. In fourth grade, she told her teacher about a distant relative who fought in Santa Anna's army at the Alamo in Texas. Her teacher, Ms. Call, decided she should not tell that story to all of the students, so Rosamaria wrote and illustrated a book about it. The teacher let her take it home to her parents instead of putting it in the school library. After that time, Rosamaria just wrote books at home or during extra time at school. She let her little sister and brother practice reading with them. Her parents were very proud of her writing and drawing.

Since third grade, Rosamaria has been in the top 25% of her class. Teachers are always happy to have Rosamaria in their class because she is polite, respectful, and works hard. Her second-grade teacher thought about nominating her for gifted services, but decided that because her first language is Spanish, she would not do well on the tests for identification. She feared that her home language might be a barrier to identification. Other teachers think Rosamaria is bright, but because she comes from such a different background, they do not think she belongs in gifted services.

Things to Consider

- *Language and cultural biases may still be present in many districts and on many campuses.*
- *Cultural differences among school populations create dilemmas for school personnel and for students.*
- *Language differences create a mismatch between the needs of students and the support from educators.*
- *Perceptions of intelligence may be clouded by a lack of understanding of language or culture.*

A New Program

The school has begun working with the RtI program. Professional development sessions are required for teachers to work on curriculum strategies in order to observe and address learning difficulties and learning strengths of students. Ms. Call, Rosamaria's teacher, has worked on the development of Level 1 curriculum that will help her observe students' learning strengths and weaknesses. The teacher of the gifted, Mr. Menzel, has added differentiation strategies to Ms. Call's curriculum so that gifted students' needs are met.

One example of an RtI Level 1 curriculum activity in Rosamaria's class is a 6-week research project for all students. Students have been cluster grouped according to interests and learning needs. Ms. Call has placed Rosamaria and two other students with the identified gifted students so that there will be six in the group and because the three nonidentified students appear to have similar interests for this project.

Rosamaria is very excited about their project. She has been able to ask questions about their topic that she has always been curious to know about and has had time and resources to explore the subject. She likes talking about the project with the other five students because they are all interested in the same things she is and all want to work hard on their project. Rosamaria makes sure that she does her part on the project, but also encourages the other two nonidentified students to complete their assignments. The identified students like working with her and are glad that she is a part of their group.

The teacher of the gifted, Mr. Menzel, has been observing the students in the room for part of the time they have been working. He is surprised that Rosamaria has never been identified for gifted services. He has noted that she learns very quickly, sees things in a different way, solves problems creatively, and is a very good leader of the other two nonidentified students. Mr. Menzel decides to ask the homeroom teacher if she will let Rosamaria stay in this cluster group for RtI Level 2 and 3 activities, for which the group will study the project more in-depth.

Ms. Call is surprised by Mr. Menzel's observation. She knows that Rosamaria is bright, but she wonders how someone from a different cultural and language background can be gifted. She has noticed that Rosamaria often responds well and effortlessly in class, but her answers reflect a different set of experiences and connections from the students who have always gone to this school. She is willing to let Rosamaria try more work with the cluster group, but she doubts that Rosamaria can handle the depth and complexity of thought required by independent study. Even though Rosamaria asks many questions and likes to probe for answers, Ms. Call just doesn't believe that Rosamaria has all of the skills that the identified gifted students already have. For example, many of the identified students have computers and Internet service at home, so that is where they often do most of their research. The identified students also often research topics that they began exploring during their summer vacation at a camp for gifted students. Ms. Call knows that Rosamaria has not had those opportunities and doesn't have a home computer, so she will have trouble keeping up with the other students.

Ms. Call decides to talk with Rosamaria's previous teachers from earlier years because she has never considered nominating students like Rosamaria. Each previous teacher says that Rosamaria is bright, but because she comes from a different culture, they did not consider her for gifted services. She thinks that she will not nominate her for gifted services because she doesn't understand how Rosamaria can handle the work of the classroom and the work differentiated for gifted students for the reasons she listed above. Ms. Call believes that Rosamaria should just keep on working at the same pace as the other students and write her books at home.

Discussion Questions

1. What characteristics of the gifted do you believe Rosamaria exhibits?
2. What are some cultural differences between middle class Anglo students and students from other cultures or with language differences?
3. What can Mr. Menzel do to help Rosamaria receive services? What can Ms. Call do to help Rosamaria excel?
4. *Standard 6: Professional Development* (see Appendix A) references building educators' knowledge and skills through professional development. In order to better understand the nature and needs of gifted learners, describe a professional development session that addresses common myths related to characteristics of the gifted from different cultures and home languages.

Activities

1. Research myths about and characteristics of giftedness in speakers of other languages. Present your findings in a product of your choice.
2. Develop a plan for identification of underrepresented populations, especially ELL/ESL/ESOL students.
3. Role-play a presentation to Rosamaria's parents about gifted services.
4. Using *Standard 6: Professional Development* (see Appendix A), develop a needs assessment for professional development that includes opportunities to understand students of different cultures, from different language backgrounds, and students of poverty.

Extensions

1. Study Slocumb and Payne's (2002) *Removing the Mask: Giftedness in Poverty*. Compare and contrast characteristics of gifted students from poverty with those of students from underrepresented populations in a graphic organizer of your choice.
2. Develop a lesson for a cluster group of gifted students to complete in an RtI Level 2 assignment, or a framework for independent study in an RtI Level 3 activity.
3. Develop a plan for your campus or district that creates professional development opportunities without extra cost to the campus/district for substitutes, that finds funds for professional development sessions, as supported in *Standard 6: Professional Development* (see Appendix A), and includes an evaluation of the effectiveness of your plan.

Additional Readings

Baum, S. (2004). *Twice-exceptional and special populations of gifted students.* Thousand Oaks, CA: Corwin Press.

Besnoy, K. D. (2006). *Successful strategies for twice-exceptional students.* Waco, TX: Prufrock Press.

Boswell, C., & Carlile, V. (2009). *Response to intervention for gifted students.* Hawthorne, NJ: Educational Impressions.

Castellano, J. A. (2003). *Special populations in gifted education: Working with diverse gifted learners.* Boston, MA: Allyn & Bacon.

Coleman, J. S., Campbell, E. Q., Hobson, C. J., McPartland, J., Mood, A. M., Weinfeld, F. D., & York, R. L. (1966). *Equality of educational opportunity* (OE-38001). Washington, DC: U.S. Government Printing Office. Retrieved from http://library.sc.edu/digital/collections/eeoci.pdf

Coleman, M. R., & Johnsen, S. K. (Eds.) (2012). *Implementing RtI with gifted students: Service models, trends, and issues.* Waco, TX: Prufrock Press.

Ford, D. Y., & Milner, H. R. (2005). *Teaching culturally diverse gifted students.* Waco, TX: Prufrock Press.

National Association for Gifted Children, & The Association for the Gifted, Council for Exceptional Children. (2006). *NAGC-CEC teacher knowledge and skill standards for gifted and talented education.* Retrieved from http://www.nagc.org/uploadedFiles/Information_and_Resources/NCATE_standards/final%20standards%20(2006).pdf

Plucker, J. A., & Callahan, C. M. (Eds.). (2008). *Critical issues and practices in gifted education: What the research says* (1st ed.). Waco, TX: Prufrock Press.

Rogers, K. B. (2002). *Re-forming gifted education: Matching the program to the child.* Scottsdale, AZ: Great Potential Press.

Texas Education Agency. (2008). *What is equity in G/T education?* Retrieved from http://www.gtequity.org/index.php

Tomlinson, C. A. (1999). *The differentiated classroom: Responding to the needs of all learners.* Alexandria, VA: ASCD.

VanTassel-Baska, J., & Stambaugh, T. (Eds.). (2007). Overlooked gems: A national perspective on low-income promising learners. *Proceedings of the National Leadership Conference on Low-Income Promising Learners* (Washington, DC, Apr 24–25, 2006). National Association for Gifted Children and the Center for Gifted Education. Retrieved from http://www.nagc.org/uploadedFiles/Publications/Overlooked%20Gems%20(password%20protected%20-%20gifted).pdf

Hendersonville Day School

Introduction

The focus of this case study is to provide the education professional with an overview of a private school's journey toward implementing differentiation in their classrooms. An introduction to the school, along with background information, leads to a relevant need to implement teaching strategies that ensure the success of all students, especially those who are capable of learning above grade level. Follow the journey that the school takes by considering the need for teacher training and staff development.

Overview of the School

- Hendersonville Day School (HDS) is an independent grade school serving students from prekindergarten through eighth grade located in an urban area.
- The school, established in the 1980s, is currently a member of a Council of Independent Schools, a Kindergarten Council, an Association of Independent Schools, and an Association of Colleges and Schools. The school has approximately 330 students, 38 faculty members, and 27 staff members.
- The mission of HDS is to provide a comprehensive and contemporary education in a moral and family-supportive environment that includes training for students in 21st-century skills, critical thinking, and informed decision making, educating students for their future.

Significant Need

Several years ago, the administration and board of HDS recognized that examining the school's strengths and weaknesses and thinking about a strategic plan were essential for meeting the needs of the students more effectively. This recognition could enhance the well-being of the organization. Months later, a handful of specific needs emerged and working committees were to be established. The Advanced Scholarship Committee, a group previously established to work with students struggling in the classroom, determined one of those needs. Although ways to more effectively support struggling students and teachers were established, the finding among students working above the grade-level curriculum was the need for more challenge. The students at HDS are a heterogeneous mix, including average students, students working below the curriculum, and students who are working above the curriculum. HDS has students classified by the formal definition of "gifted." About 5% of the school population is identified as gifted with an IQ of 130 or greater.

Although the administration understood and implemented differentiation, they were interested in helping the faculty do the same. It was decided that an outside expert was needed to help guide the process of implementing differentiation in the classrooms. Contact with an expert was established and the process began.

Things to Consider

- *There are different perceptions for what differentiating curriculum and instruction means.*
- *Multiple strategies can be used to differentiate curriculum and instruction.*
- *There are different barriers to overcome when creating a school climate for differentiation.*
- *Differentiated instruction provides opportunities for matching the students' instructional needs with the curriculum.*

The administrators understood differentiation based on their own background and training in special education. They also realized the need for faculty to have staff development on differentiated curriculum and instruction. A plan would need to be developed that would empower the teachers to differentiate in their own classrooms. A preassessment survey was used to identify any misconceptions from the faculty related to differentiation. These misconceptions included believing that differentiation is only for students needing special education or that differentiation is far too complicated and challenging for the general educator to implement. Additional misconceptions included the idea that differentiation is a different lesson plan for each student. It appeared that the teachers initially had little understanding of the types of differentiation strategies for high-ability and gifted students, and as a result, were reluctant to offer very much input.

Discussion Questions

1. What are some specific and universal needs that private and/or charter schools share with public schools regarding implementing services for gifted learners?

2. What are the major concerns with promoting systemic change that leads to differentiation? Are they valid concerns? Why or why not?

3. What do the elements of a differentiated classroom look like? Sound like? According to what or whom?

4. How might leadership impede and/or support the implementation of differentiation? What are the characteristics of effective staff development on differentiation?

5. How do professional development goals and student performance outcomes relate?

Activities

1. *Evidence-Based Practices 6.1* references professional development for educators of gifted learners (see Appendix A). What attributes affect the quality of professional development? Create a pitch to your principal or school board about the need for training fellow educators about the nature and needs of gifted learners.

2. What knowledge, skills, and dispositions do teachers need to manage a differentiated classroom? Create a preassessment survey to determine teachers' level of understanding related to classroom management for differentiated instruction.

3. Make a list of the major barriers to overcome when implementing school-wide differentiated instruction. How can you prioritize this list? Discuss with a partner the various ways to overcome these obstacles.

4. Explore various philosophies and approaches related to differentiated instruction (e.g., Tomlinson, Roberts, Heacox, Coil, etc.). What are the advantages and disadvantages of each? Write a recommendation for implementing a philosophy or philosophies

5. What are the key elements of staff development that supports differentiation? Develop the next steps in planning and implementing staff development for differentiation.

6. Brainstorm the qualities of effective communication with parents and the public about differentiation. Develop a set of guidelines for coordinators/administrators new to the gifted field

7. What are the next steps for Hendersonville Day School to consider? What resources may be available through the National Charter School Resource Center? Outline a brief plan of action.

Extensions

1. Study various models for professional development (e.g., Guskey, distance education, Javits Grant Model, etc.) such as those found in the *NAGC*

Pre-K–Grade 12 Gifted Education Programming Standards: A Guide to Planning and Implementing High-Quality Services (Johnsen, 2012). Using a matrix, identify similar and different components found in each one.

2. How can you suggest teachers be held accountable for implementing differentiation in their classrooms? Research tools designed to assess teachers' implementation of differentiated curriculum and instruction and write a short review of each one.

Additional Readings

Cash, R. M. (2011). *Advancing differentiation: Thinking and learning for the 21st century.* Minneapolis, MN: Free Spirit.

Coil, C. (2007). *Successful teaching in the differentiated classroom.* Marion, IL: Pieces of Learning.

Heacox, D. (2002). *Differentiating instruction in the regular classroom: How to reach and teach all learners, grades 3–12.* Minneapolis, MN: Free Spirit.

Heacox, D. (2009). *Making differentiation a habit: How to ensure success in academically diverse classrooms.* Minneapolis, MN: Free Spirit.

Johnsen, S. K. (Ed.). (2012). *NAGC Pre-K–Grade 12 gifted education programming standards: A guide to planning and implementing high-quality services.* Waco, TX: Prufrock Press.

Kingore, B. (2004). *Differentiation: Simplified, realistic, and effective.* Austin, TX: Professional Associates.

National Association for Gifted Children. (2010). *Pre-K–Grade 12 gifted education programming standards.* Retrieved from http://www.nagc.org/index.aspx?id=546

O'Meara, J. (2010). *Beyond differentiated instruction.* Thousand Oaks, CA: Corwin Press.

Roberts, J. L., & Inman, T. F. (2009). *Strategies for differentiating instruction: Best practices for the classroom.* Waco, TX: Prufrock Press.

Tomlinson, C. A., & Allan, S. D. (2000). *Leadership for differentiating schools and classroom.* Alexandria, VA: ASCD.

Tomlinson, C. A., Brimijoin, K., & Narvaez, L. (2008). *The differentiated school: Making revolutionary changes in teaching and learning.* Alexandria, VA: ASCD.

Tomlinson, C. A., & Imbeau, M. B. (2010). *Leading and managing a differentiated classroom.* Alexandria, VA: ASCD.

University School District

Introduction

Change in delivery of services for gifted and talented students from once-a-week pull-out classes to in-class cluster grouping requires long-term, in-depth professional development to ensure appropriate services for students. Teachers must change from meeting the needs of a wide variety of students to creating a learning environment for those who learn more quickly and desire to learn in greater depth and with more complexity.

This case, University School District (USD), centers on the administrative and teaching professionals' involvement in professional development to create classrooms for gifted and advanced learners.

USD

University School District is a mid-sized district of 20,000 students. There are 20 elementary campuses equally distributed across the north, south, east, and west sectors of Rayder City. The elementary campuses include 500–650 students from prekindergarten through fifth grade.

Although a part of the decision to move from pull-out to in-class cluster classrooms services is monetary, the ultimate goal is that gifted and advanced students learn in environments that meet their needs on a daily basis, rather than once each week. One issue stemming from this change relates to the number of teachers and their administrators who must participate in professional development within the monetary and time constraints of the district. District administrators recognize that other issues may surface throughout the first year of implementation, but their efforts will center on professional development.

> ## Things to Consider
>
> - *Administrators need to support teachers in cluster classrooms.*
> - *Teacher selection should be based on individuals' knowledge of the needs of gifted and advanced learners and the curriculum appropriate for this population.*
> - *Campus and individual Professional Development Plans (PDP) are developed based on formal and informal observations of teachers and students.*
> - *Professional development should be delivered in a variety of formats.*

The Campuses

The campuses in USD can be divided into categories that range from meeting needs of all learners to meeting needs of only struggling learners. Three campus types fall into the categories below.

Type 1 campuses understand and meet the needs of gifted and advanced learners through highly qualified teachers and with curriculum appropriate for gifted learners. They include many teachers with master's degrees in gifted education who are able to meet the needs of all learners on their campus. These teachers regularly participate in professional development. Their campuses focus on project- and problem-based learning, infusing critical and creative thinking into all lessons. Their teachers and administrators consistently search for new ways to meet the needs of all learners on their campuses. Classrooms are designed with learning centers and other physical arrangements that allow for differentiation.

Type 2 campuses have knowledge of this population's needs, but historically have left all curriculum efforts to the pull-out teachers. Fewer teachers have sought advanced degrees in gifted education. Very often, their campus professional development revolves around the needs of struggling learners who need help with basic skills. Their focus is on Reponse to Intervention (RtI) for the needs of the learning disabled, dyslexic, and students who have difficulty with basic math and reading skills. They often use gifted students to tutor learners who need help in math and reading.

Type 3 campuses only meet the needs of those learners who struggle to grasp basic content; therefore, leaving gifted learners to learn on their own or act as tutors for other students. Type 3 campus teachers feel they must only meet the needs of those learners who struggle to grasp basic content and are similar to the Type 2 campuses in their approach to services for gifted and talented students. The teachers and administrators are angry that there is no longer one teacher on each campus to serve this population. For example, all identification procedures, extracurricular and cocurricular competitions, and field experiences were previously the responsibility of the pull-out teacher. With that teacher now in a regular or cluster classroom, the administrator must struggle to find another person to take over the tasks or require that each cluster teacher take his or her share of the responsibility.

The Challenge

The Director of Advanced Academic Services must make a plan to encompass all PD needs so that gifted and talented students have opportunities to work at their required level of learning, at an appropriate pace of curriculum, and interact with other gifted students (Latz, Speirs Neumeister, Adams, & Pierce; 2009; McDiarmid & Clevenger-Bright, 2008; VanTassel-Baska, 2006).

Many campus' leaders, teachers, and parents are unhappy with the change in delivery of services. Most were content to see the children work on projects of varying quality in a segregated environment. Parents' uneasiness ranges from the fear that their child will not receive the level of instruction they feel is necessary to the fear that their children will have to become teacher aides in the mixed-ability classroom.

Campus leaders recognize their job will encompass the "how-to" for the first year: how to meet students' needs, how to develop curriculum, and how to manage classrooms teachers' concerns related to differentiated curriculum. They realize they have not developed curriculum specifically for the pace and depth required for gifted and talented learners. University School District administrators, the Superintendent of USD, the Assistant Superintendent for Curriculum and Instruction, and the Director of Advanced Academic Services have tried to allay all fears by stating that their gifted and talented children will receive quality services all day, every day instead of once a week. This core of administrators also realizes that a considerable amount of PD must be offered in order to meet the expectations of the parents and community. The professional development must include curriculum development, an understanding of the nature and needs of gifted students, and classroom management to facilitate differentiation (Hertberg-Davis & Brighton 2006; Johnsen, Haensly, Ryser, & Ford, 2002; NAGC, 2010; VanTassel-Baska & Stambaugh, 2005).

School district personnel look to the *NAGC Pre-K–Grade 12 Gifted Programming Standards* (2010; see Appendix A) for guidance in meeting the needs of students in USD elementary schools. Within *Standard 1: Learning and Development,* they explore *Student Outcomes* and *Evidence-Based Practices* (see Appendix A) in order to establish the best possible learning environment for the students.

Discussion Questions

1. Are all campuses easily divided in the three categories? How could your district divide its campuses?
2. What needs beyond professional development could be considered?
3. Is professional development the only way to help teachers customize instruction for gifted learners? Why or why not?
4. In what other ways could the needs of the teachers' be described? How can their needs be met?
5. If your state uses a prescribed teacher evaluation tool, in what ways could this case study use it?
6. In what ways does your state or district use an evaluation tool for professional development?

Activities

1. Use *Evidence-Based Practice 1.3.1* (see Appendix A) to develop a 3-hour professional development session for one of the campuses described in this case. Present this to your faculty if appropriate.
2. Describe at least two other means of facilitating the delivery of services for gifted children in one of the campuses mentioned above. Create a role-play for a faculty meeting.
3. Select a Type 2 or 3 classroom described in this case. Detail and illustrate how you believe the classroom would look physically. Make changes to the classroom to meet *Standard 1: Learning and Development Evidence-Based Practices 1.1.1 and 1.1.2* (see Appendix A).
4. Research the best practices among those in *Standard 1: Learning and Development Evidence-Based Practices 1.3.1.* (see Appendix A). Develop one activity to facilitate a practice within a classroom in a Type 3 campus.

Extensions

1. Create a chart that compares and contrasts the positive and negative aspects of pull-out services for gifted learners versus cluster classrooms.
2. Develop an online 3-hour professional development session on the topic of classroom management for G/T students in the regular classroom. Offer the session to your district or a regional education group.
3. Create a board of education presentation that describes the purpose of cluster classrooms for gifted learners or the advantages of pull-out services for gifted students.

Additional Readings

Brighton, C. M., & Moon, T. R. (2007, November). *Two decades of research on differentiation: What do we now know?* Presentation at the National Association for Gifted Children Annual Professional Development Conference, Minneapolis, MN. Retrieved from http://nrcgtuva.org/presentations/Two DecadesofResearch_CMBTRM2007.pdf

Colangelo, N., Assouline, S. G., & Gross, M. U. M. (2004). *A nation deceived: How schools hold back America's brightest students* (Vol. 1) Iowa City: University of Iowa, The Connie Belin & Jacqueline N. Blank International Center for Gifted Education and Talent Development. Retrieved from http://www.education.uiowa.edu/belinblank/pdfs/ND_v1.pdf

Council of Chief State School Officers. (2011, April). *Interstate Teacher Assessment and Support Consortium model core teaching standards: A resource for state dialogue.* Washington, DC: Author.

Edgecombe, N. (2011). *Accelerating the academic achievement of students referred to developmental education* [CCRC Working Paper No. 30]. New York, NY: Community College Research Center, Teachers College, Columbia University. Retrieved from http://ccrc.tc.columbia.edu/Publication.asp?UID=867

Knopper, D., & Fertig, C. (2005). Differentiation for gifted children: It's all about trust. *The Illinois Association for Gifted Children Journal, 6*(1), 6–8.

National Governors Association. (2009, December). *Increasing college success: A road map for governors* [Issue Brief]. Washington, DC: NGA Center for Best Practices.

Paul, R., & Elder, L. (2009). *The miniature guide to critical thinking: Concepts and tools.* Tomales, CA: Foundation for Critical Thinking Press.

References

Astuto, T. A., Clark, D. L., Read, A.-M., McGree, K., & Fernandez, L. de K. P. (1993). *Challenges to dominant assumptions controlling educational reform.* Andover, MA: Regional Laboratory for the Educational Improvement of the Northeast and Islands.

Baum, S. (2004). *Twice-exceptional and special populations of gifted students.* Thousand Oaks, CA: Corwin Press.

Burkman, A. (2012). Preparing novice teachers for success in elementary classrooms though professional development. *The Delta Kappa Gamma Bulletin, 78*(3), 23–33.

Cash, R. M. (2011). *Advancing differentiation: Thinking and learning for the 21st century.* Minneapolis, MN: Free Spirit.

Cavanaugh, C., & Dawson, K. (2010). Design of online professional development in science content and pedagogy: A pilot study in Florida. *Journal of Science Education and Technology,* 438–446.

Colangelo, N., Assouline, S. G., & Gross, M. U. M. (2004). *A nation deceived: How schools hold back America's brightest students* (Vol. 1). Iowa City: University of Iowa, The Connie Belin & Jacqueline N. Blank International Center for Gifted Education and Talent Development. Retrieved from http://www.education.uiowa.edu/belinblank/pdfs/ND_v1.pdf

Council of Chief State School Officers. (2011, April). *InTASC model core teaching standards: A resource for state dialogue.* Retrieved from http://www.ccsso.org/Documents/2011/InTASC_Model_Core_Teaching_Standards_2011.pdf

Dawson, K., Cavanaugh, C., & Ritzhaupt, A. (2012). ARTI: An online tool to support teacher action research for technology integration. In R. Hartshorne, T. Heafner, & T. Petty (Eds.), *Teacher education programs and online learn-*

ing tools: Innovations in teacher preparation (pp. 375–391). Hershey, PA: IGI Global.

Dawson, K., Cavanaugh, C., Sessums, C., Black, E., & Kumar, S. (2011). Designing a professional practice doctoral degree in educational technology: Signature pedagogies, implications and recommendations. *Journal of Distance Education, 25*(3). Retrieved from http://www.jofde.ca/index.php/jde/article/view/767/1317

Dwyer, D. C., Ringstaff, C., & Sandholtz, J. H. (1991). Changes in teachers' beliefs and practices in technology-rich classrooms. *Educational Leadership, 48*(8), 45–52.

Finkle, S. L., & Torp, L. L. (1995). *Introductory documents.* Aurora, IL: The Center for Problem-Based Learning, Illinois Math and Science Academy.

Hertberg-Davis, H. L., & Brighton, C. M. (2006). Support and sabotage: Principals' influence on middle school teachers' responses to differentiation. *Journal of Secondary Gifted Education, 17,* 90–102. doi:10.4219/jsge-2006-685

Hooper, S., & Rieber, L. P. (1995). Teaching with technology. In A. C. Ornstein (Ed.), *Teaching: Theory into practice* (pp. 154–170). Needham Heights, MA: Allyn & Bacon.

Hord, S. M. (1997). Professional learning communities: What are they and why are they important? *Issues About Change, 6*(1), 1–8. Retrieved from http://www.sedl.org/change/issues/issues61.html

Johnsen, S. K. (2005). *Identifying gifted students: A step-by-step guide.* Waco, TX: Prufrock Press.

Johnsen, S. K. (Ed.). (2012). *NAGC Pre-K–Grade 12 gifted education programming standards: A guide to planning and implementing high-quality services.* Waco, TX: Prufrock Press.

Johnsen, S. K., Haensly, P. A., Ryser, G. R., & Ford, R. F. (2002). Changing general education classroom practices to adapt for gifted students. *Gifted Child Quarterly, 46*(1), 45–63. doi:10.1177/001698620204600105

Kordosky, D. L. (2011). Attending to the gifted in rural schools. *School Administrator, 68*(8), 42–43. Retrieved from http://www.aasa.org/SchoolAdministrator.aspx

Kumar, S., Dawson, K., Black, E. W., Cavanaugh, C., & Sessums, C. D. (2011). Applying the Community of Inquiry framework to an online professional practice doctoral program. *International Review of Research in Open and Distance Learning, 12,* 126–142.

Kuntz, S., & Hessler, A. (1998, January). *Bridging the gap between theory and practice: Fostering active learning through the case method.* Paper presented at the Annual Meeting of the Association of American Colleges and Universities, Washington, DC. Retrieved from (ED420626)

Landrum, M. S., Callahan, C. M., & Shaklee, B. D. (2001). *Aiming for excellence: Annotations to the NAGC Pre-K–Grade 12 gifted program standards.* Waco, TX: Prufrock Press.

Latz, A. O., Speirs Neumeister, K. L., Adams, C. M., & Pierce, R. L. (2009). Peer coaching to improve classroom differentiation: Perspectives from Project CLUE. *Roeper Review, 31*(1), 27–39. doi:10.1080/02783190802527356

McDiarmid, G. W., & Clevenger-Bright, M. (2008). Rethinking teacher capacity. In M. Cochran-Smith, S. Feiman-Nemser, D. J. McIntyre, & K. E. Demers (Eds.), *Handbook of research on teacher education: Enduring questions in changing contexts* (3rd ed., pp. 134–156). New York, NY: Routledge.

McKnight, K. S. (2010). *The teacher's big book of graphic organizers, grades 5–12.* San Francisco, CA: Jossey-Bass.

Moersch, C. (1995). Levels of technology implementation (LoTi): A framework for measuring classroom technology use. *Learning and Leading with Technology, 23*(3), 40–42. Retrieved from http://webpages.csus.edu/~ML3226/edte281/LOTIFrameworkNov95.pdf

National Association for Gifted Children. (2008). *Redefining giftedness for a new century: Shifting the paradigm* [Position paper]. Retrieved from http://www.nagc.org/index.aspx?id=6404

National Association for Gifted Children. (2010). *Pre-K–Grade 12 gifted education programming standards.* Retrieved from http://www.nagc.org/index.aspx?id=546

National Association for Gifted Children, & Council for Exceptional Children, The Association for the Gifted. (2006). *NAGC-CEC teacher knowledge and skill standards for gifted and talented education.* Retrieved from http://www.ncate.org/Standards/ProgramStandardsandReportForms/tabid/676/Default.aspx

National Board for Professional Teaching Standards. (2011). *Exceptional needs standards* (2nd ed.). Retrieved from http://www.nbpts.org/for_candidates/certificate_areas1?ID=18&x=42&y=9

National Staff Development Council. (2011). *Standards for professional learning.* Retrieved from http://www.learningforward.org/index.cfm

National Research Center on Rural Education Support. *Mission.* (n.d.). Retrieved from http://www.nrcres.org/index.html

Olszewski-Kubilius, P., & Clarenbach, J. (2012). *Unlocking emergent talent: Supporting high achievement of low-income, high ability students.* Washington, DC: National Association for Gifted Children. Retrieved from http://www.nagc.org/uploadedfiles/Conventions_and_seminars/National_Research_Summit/Unlocking%20Emergent%20Talent%20Full%20No-Tint.pdf

Passow, A. H. (1996). Acceleration over the years. In C. P. Benbow & D. Lubinski (Eds.), *Intellectual talent: Psychometric and social issues* (pp. 93–98). Baltimore, MD: Johns Hopkins University Press.

Rogers, K. B. (2002). *Re-forming gifted education: Matching the program to the child.* Scottsdale, AZ: Great Potential Press.

Silverman, L. K. (1993). *Counseling the gifted and talented.* Denver, CO: Love Publishing.

Slocumb, P. D., & Payne, R. K. (2000). *Removing the mask: Giftedness in poverty.* Highlands, TX: Aha! Process.

Stepien, W., & Gallagher, S. (1993, April). Problem-based learning: As authentic as it gets. *Educational Leadership, 50*(7), 25–28.

Swartz, R. J., & Parks, S. (1994). *Infusing the teaching of critical and creative thinking into content instruction: A lesson design handbook for the elementary grades.* Pacific Grove, CA: Critical Thinking Books & Software.

U.S. Census Bureau. (2003). *Census Bureau releases population estimates by age, sex, race and Hispanic origin.* Retrieved from http://www.census.gov/population/hispanic/data/2003.html

VanTassel-Baska, J. (2006). A content analysis of evaluation findings across 20 gifted programs: A clarion call for enhanced gifted program development. *Gifted Child Quarterly, 50,* 199–215. doi:10.1177/001698620605000302

VanTassel-Baska, J., & Stambaugh, T. (2005). Challenges and possibilities for serving gifted learners in the regular classroom. *Theory Into Practice, 44,* 211–217. doi:10.1207/s15430421tip4403_5

Appendix A

NAGC PreK–Grade 12 Gifted Education Programming Standards

Gifted Education Programming Standard 1: Learning and Development

Introduction

To be effective in working with learners with gifts and talents, teachers and other educators in PreK–12 settings must understand the characteristics and needs of the population for whom they are planning curriculum, instruction, assessment, programs, and services. These characteristics provide the rationale for differentiation in programs, grouping, and services for this population and are translated into appropriate differentiation choices made at curricular and program levels in schools and school districts. While cognitive growth is important in such programs, affective development is also necessary. Thus many of the characteristics addressed in this standard emphasize affective development linked to self-understanding and social awareness.

Standard 1: Learning and Development

Description: Educators, recognizing the learning and developmental differences of students with gifts and talents, promote ongoing self-understanding, awareness of their needs, and cognitive and affective growth of these students in school, home, and community settings to ensure specific student outcomes.

Student Outcomes	Evidence-Based Practices
1.1. Self-Understanding. Students with gifts and talents demonstrate self-knowledge with respect to their interests, strengths, identities, and needs in socio-emotional development and in intellectual, academic, creative, leadership, and artistic domains.	1.1.1. Educators engage students with gifts and talents in identifying interests, strengths, and gifts. 1.1.2. Educators assist students with gifts and talents in developing identities supportive of achievement.
1.2. Self-Understanding. Students with gifts and talents possess a developmentally appropriate understanding of how they learn and grow; they recognize the influences of their beliefs, traditions, and values on their learning and behavior.	1.2.1. Educators develop activities that match each student's developmental level and culture-based learning needs.
1.3. Self-Understanding. Students with gifts and talents demonstrate understanding of and respect for similarities and differences between themselves and their peer group and others in the general population.	1.3.1. Educators provide a variety of research-based grouping practices for students with gifts and talents that allow them to interact with individuals of various gifts, talents, abilities, and strengths. 1.3.2. Educators model respect for individuals with diverse abilities, strengths, and goals.
1.4. Awareness of Needs. Students with gifts and talents access resources from the community to support cognitive and affective needs, including social interactions with others having similar interests and abilities or experiences, including same-age peers and mentors or experts.	1.4.1. Educators provide role models (e.g., through mentors, bibliotherapy) for students with gifts and talents that match their abilities and interests. 1.4.2. Educators identify out-of-school learning opportunities that match students' abilities and interests.
1.5. Awareness of Needs. Students' families and communities understand similarities and differences with respect to the development and characteristics of advanced and typical learners and support students with gifts and talents' needs.	1.5.1. Educators collaborate with families in accessing resources to develop their child's talents.
1.6. Cognitive and Affective Growth. Students with gifts and talents benefit from meaningful and challenging learning activities addressing their unique characteristics and needs.	1.6.1. Educators design interventions for students to develop cognitive and affective growth that is based on research of effective practices. 1.6.2. Educators develop specialized intervention services for students with gifts and talents who are underachieving and are now learning and developing their talents.

Student Outcomes	Evidence-Based Practices
1.7. Cognitive and Affective Growth. Students with gifts and talents recognize their preferred approaches to learning and expand their repertoire.	1.7.1. Teachers enable students to identify their preferred approaches to learning, accommodate these preferences, and expand them.
1.8. Cognitive and Affective Growth. Students with gifts and talents identify future career goals that match their talents and abilities and resources needed to meet those goals (e.g., higher education opportunities, mentors, financial support).	1.8.1. Educators provide students with college and career guidance that is consistent with their strengths. 1.8.2. Teachers and counselors implement a curriculum scope and sequence that contains person/social awareness and adjustment, academic planning, and vocational and career awareness.

Gifted Education Programming Standard 2: Assessment

Introduction

Knowledge about all forms of assessment is essential for educators of students with gifts and talents. It is integral to identification, assessing each student's learning progress, and evaluation of programming. Educators need to establish a challenging environment and collect multiple types of assessment information so that all students are able to demonstrate their gifts and talents. Educators' understanding of non-biased, technically adequate, and equitable approaches enables them to identify students who represent diverse backgrounds. They also differentiate their curriculum and instruction by using pre- and post-, performance-based, product-based, and out-of-level assessments. As a result of each educator's use of ongoing assessments, students with gifts and talents demonstrate advanced and complex learning. Using these student progress data, educators then evaluate services and make adjustments to one or more of the school's programming components so that student performance is improved.

Standard 2: Assessment

Description: Assessments provide information about identification, learning progress and outcomes, and evaluation of programming for students with gifts and talents in all domains.

Student Outcomes	Evidence-Based Practices
2.1. Identification. All students in grades PK–12 have equal access to a comprehensive assessment system that allows them to demonstrate diverse characteristics and behaviors that are associated with giftedness.	2.1.1. Educators develop environments and instructional activities that encourage students to express diverse characteristics and behaviors that are associated with giftedness. 2.1.2. Educators provide parents/guardians with information regarding diverse characteristics and behaviors that are associated with giftedness.
2.2. Identification. Each student reveals his or her exceptionalities or potential through assessment evidence so that appropriate instructional accommodations and modifications can be provided.	2.2.1. Educators establish comprehensive, cohesive, and ongoing procedures for identifying and serving students with gifts and talents. These provisions include informed consent, committee review, student retention, student reassessment, student exiting, and appeals procedures for both entry and exit from gifted program services.
	2.2.2. Educators select and use multiple assessments that measure diverse abilities, talents, and strengths that are based on current theories, models, and research. 2.2.3 Assessments provide qualitative and quantitative information from a variety of sources, including off-level testing, are nonbiased and equitable, and are technically adequate for the purpose. 2.2.4. Educators have knowledge of student exceptionalities and collect assessment data while adjusting curriculum and instruction to learn about each student's developmental level and aptitude for learning. 2.2.5. Educators interpret multiple assessments in different domains and understand the uses and limitations of the assessments in identifying the needs of students with gifts and talents. 2.2.6. Educators inform all parents/guardians about the identification process. Teachers obtain parental/guardian permission for assessments, use culturally sensitive checklists, and elicit evidence regarding the child's interests and potential outside of the classroom setting.

Student Outcomes	Evidence-Based Practices
2.3. Identification. Students with identified needs represent diverse backgrounds and reflect the total student population of the district.	2.3.1. Educators select and use non-biased and equitable approaches for identifying students with gifts and talents, which may include using locally developed norms or assessment tools in the child's native language or in nonverbal formats. 2.3.2. Educators understand and implement district and state policies designed to foster equity in gifted programming and services. 2.3.3. Educators provide parents/ guardians with information in their native language regarding diverse behaviors and characteristics that are associated with giftedness and with information that explains the nature and purpose of gifted programming options.
2.4. Learning Progress and Outcomes. Students with gifts and talents demonstrate advanced and complex learning as a result of using multiple, appropriate, and ongoing assessments.	2.4.1. Educators use differentiated pre- and post- performance-based assessments to measure the progress of students with gifts and talents. 2.4.2. Educators use differentiated product-based assessments to measure the progress of students with gifts and talents.
	2.4.3. Educators use off-level standardized assessments to measure the progress of students with gifts and talents. 2.4.4. Educators use and interpret qualitative and quantitative assessment information to develop a profile of the strengths and weaknesses of each student with gifts and talents to plan appropriate intervention. 2.4.5. Educators communicate and interpret assessment information to students with gifts and talents and their parents/guardians.

Student Outcomes	Evidence-Based Practices
2.5. Evaluation of Programming. Students identified with gifts and talents demonstrate important learning progress as a result of programming and services.	2.5.1. Educators ensure that the assessments used in the identification and evaluation processes are reliable and valid for each instrument's purpose, allow for above-grade-level performance, and allow for diverse perspectives. 2.5.2. Educators ensure that the assessment of the progress of students with gifts and talents uses multiple indicators that measure mastery of content, higher level thinking skills, achievement in specific program areas, and affective growth. 2.5.3. Educators assess the quantity, quality, and appropriateness of the programming and services provided for students with gifts and talents by disaggregating assessment data and yearly progress data and making the results public.
2.6. Evaluation of Programming. Students identified with gifts and talents have increased access and they show significant learning progress as a result of improving components of gifted education programming.	2.6.1. Administrators provide the necessary time and resources to implement an annual evaluation plan developed by persons with expertise in program evaluation and gifted education. 2.6.2. The evaluation plan is purposeful and evaluates how student-level outcomes are influenced by one or more of the following components of gifted education programming: (a) identification, (b) curriculum, (c) instructional programming and services, (d) ongoing assessment of student learning, (e) counseling and guidance programs, (f) teacher qualifications and professional development, (g) parent/guardian and community involvement, (h) programming resources, and (i) programming design, management, and delivery. 2.6.3. Educators disseminate the results of the evaluation, orally and in written form, and explain how they will use the results.

Gifted Education Programming Standard 3: Curriculum Planning and Instruction

Introduction

Assessment is an integral component of the curriculum planning process. The information obtained from multiple types of assessments informs decisions about curriculum content, instructional strategies, and resources that will support the growth of students with gifts and talents. Educators develop and use a comprehensive and sequenced core curriculum that is aligned with local, state, and national standards, then differentiate and expand it. In order to meet the unique needs of students with gifts and talents, this curriculum must emphasize advanced, conceptually challenging, in-depth, distinctive, and complex content within cognitive, affective, aesthetic, social, and leadership domains. Educators must possess a repertoire of evidence-based instructional strategies in delivering the curriculum (a) to develop talent, enhance learning, and provide students with the knowledge and skills to become independent, self-aware learners, and (b) to give students the tools to contribute to a multicultural, diverse society. The curriculum, instructional strategies, and materials and resources must engage a variety of learners using culturally responsive practices.

Standard 3: Curriculum Planning and Instruction
Description: Educators apply the theory and research-based models of curriculum and instruction related to students with gifts and talents and respond to their needs by planning, selecting, adapting, and creating culturally relevant curriculum and by using a repertoire of evidence-based instructional strategies to ensure specific student outcomes.

Student Outcomes	Evidence-Based Practices
3.1. Curriculum Planning. Students with gifts and talents demonstrate growth commensurate with aptitude during the school year.	3.1.1. Educators use local, state, and national standards to align and expand curriculum and instructional plans. 3.1.2. Educators design and use a comprehensive and continuous scope and sequence to develop differentiated plans for PK–12 students with gifts and talents. 3.1.3. Educators adapt, modify, or replace the core or standard curriculum to meet the needs of students with gifts and talents and those with special needs such as twice-exceptional, highly gifted, and English language learners.

Student Outcomes	Evidence-Based Practices
	3.1.4. Educators design differentiated curricula that incorporate advanced, conceptually challenging, in-depth, distinctive, and complex content for students with gifts and talents. 3.1.5. Educators use a balanced assessment system, including pre-assessment and formative assessment, to identify students' needs, develop differentiated education plans, and adjust plans based on continual progress monitoring. 3.1.6. Educators use pre-assessments and pace instruction based on the learning rates of students with gifts and talents and accelerate and compact learning as appropriate. 3.1.7. Educators use information and technologies, including assistive technologies, to individualize for students with gifts and talents, including those who are twice-exceptional.
3.2. Talent Development. Students with gifts and talents become more competent in multiple talent areas and across dimensions of learning.	3.2.1. Educators design curricula in cognitive, affective, aesthetic, social, and leadership domains that are challenging and effective for students with gifts and talents. 3.2.2. Educators use metacognitive models to meet the needs of students with gifts and talents.
3.3. Talent Development. Students with gifts and talents develop their abilities in their domain of talent and/or area of interest.	3.3.1. Educators select, adapt, and use a repertoire of instructional strategies and materials that differentiate for students with gifts and talents and that respond to diversity. 3.3.2. Educators use school and community resources that support differentiation. 3.3.3. Educators provide opportunities for students with gifts and talents to explore, develop, or research their areas of interest and/or talent.

Student Outcomes	Evidence-Based Practices
3.4. Instructional Strategies. Students with gifts and talents become independent investigators.	3.4.1. Educators use critical-thinking strategies to meet the needs of students with gifts and talents. 3.4.2. Educators use creative-thinking strategies to meet the needs of students with gifts and talents. 3.4.3. Educators use problem-solving model strategies to meet the needs of students with gifts and talents. 3.4.4. Educators use inquiry models to meet the needs of students with gifts and talents.
3.5. Culturally Relevant Curriculum. Students with gifts and talents develop knowledge and skills for living and being productive in a multicultural, diverse, and global society.	3.5.1. Educators develop and use challenging, culturally responsive curriculum to engage all students with gifts and talents. 3.5.2. Educators integrate career exploration experiences into learning opportunities for students with gifts and talents, e.g. biography study or speakers. 3.5.3. Educators use curriculum for deep explorations of cultures, languages, and social issues related to diversity.
3.6. Resources. Students with gifts and talents benefit from gifted education programming that provides a variety of high quality resources and materials.	3.6.1. Teachers and administrators demonstrate familiarity with sources for high quality resources and materials that are appropriate for learners with gifts and talents.

Gifted Education Programming Standard 4: Learning Environments

Introduction

Effective educators of students with gifts and talents create safe learning environments that foster emotional well-being, positive social interaction, leadership for social change, and cultural understanding for success in a diverse society. Knowledge of the impact of giftedness and diversity on social-emotional development enables educators of students with gifts and talents to design environments that encourage independence, motivation, and self-efficacy of individuals from all backgrounds. They understand the role of language and communication in talent development and the ways in which culture affects communication and behavior. They use relevant strategies and technologies to enhance oral, written, and artistic communication of learners whose needs vary based on exceptionality, language proficiency, and cultural and linguistic differences. They recognize the value of multilingualism in today's global community.

Standard 4: Learning Environments

Description: Learning environments foster personal and social responsibility, multicultural competence, and interpersonal and technical communication skills for leadership in the 21st century to ensure specific student outcomes.

Student Outcomes	Evidence-Based Practices
4.1. Personal Competence. Students with gifts and talents demonstrate growth in personal competence and dispositions for exceptional academic and creative productivity. These include self-awareness, self-advocacy, self-efficacy, confidence, motivation, resilience, independence, curiosity, and risk taking.	4.1.1. Educators maintain high expectations for all students with gifts and talents as evidenced in meaningful and challenging activities. 4.1.2. Educators provide opportunities for self-exploration, development and pursuit of interests, and development of identities supportive of achievement, e.g., through mentors and role models. 4.1.3. Educators create environments that support trust among diverse learners. 4.1.4. Educators provide feedback that focuses on effort, on evidence of potential to meet high standards, and on mistakes as learning opportunities. 4.1.5. Educators provide examples of positive coping skills and opportunities to apply them.
4.2. Social Competence. Students with gifts and talents develop social competence manifested in positive peer relationships and social interactions.	4.2.1. Educators understand the needs of students with gifts and talents for both solitude and social interaction. 4.2.2. Educators provide opportunities for interaction with intellectual and artistic/creative peers as well as with chronological-age peers. 4.2.3. Educators assess and provide instruction on social skills needed for school, community, and the world of work.
4.3. Leadership. Students with gifts and talents demonstrate personal and social responsibility and leadership skills.	4.3.1. Educators establish a safe and welcoming climate for addressing social issues and developing personal responsibility. 4.3.2. Educators provide environments for developing many forms of leadership and leadership skills. 4.3.3. Educators promote opportunities for leadership in community settings to effect positive change.

Student Outcomes	Evidence-Based Practices
4.4. Cultural Competence. Students with gifts and talents value their own and others' language, heritage, and circumstance. They possess skills in communicating, teaming, and collaborating with diverse individuals and across diverse groups.[1] They use positive strategies to address social issues, including discrimination and stereotyping.	4.4.1. Educators model appreciation for and sensitivity to students' diverse backgrounds and languages. 4.4.2. Educators censure discriminatory language and behavior and model appropriate strategies. 4.4.3. Educators provide structured opportunities to collaborate with diverse peers on a common goal.
4.5. Communication Competence. Students with gifts and talents develop competence in interpersonal and technical communication skills. They demonstrate advanced oral and written skills, balanced biliteracy or multiliteracy, and creative expression. They display fluency with technologies that support effective communication	4.5.1. Educators provide opportunities for advanced development and maintenance of first and second language(s). 4.5.2. Educators provide resources to enhance oral, written, and artistic forms of communication, recognizing students' cultural context. 4.5.3. Educators ensure access to advanced communication tools, including assistive technologies, and use of these tools for expressing higher-level thinking and creative productivity.

1   Differences among groups of people and individuals based on ethnicity, race, socioeconomic status, gender, exceptionalities, language, religion, sexual orientation, and geographical area.

Gifted Education Programming Standard 5: Programming

Introduction

The term programming refers to a continuum of services that address students with gifts and talents' needs in all settings. Educators develop policies and procedures to guide and sustain all components of comprehensive and aligned programming and services for PreK-12 students with gifts and talents. Educators use a variety of programming options such as acceleration and enrichment in varied grouping arrangements (cluster grouping, resource rooms, special classes, special schools) and within individualized learning options (independent study, mentorships, online courses, internships) to enhance students' performance in cognitive and affective areas and to assist them in identifying future career goals. They augment and integrate current technologies within these learning opportunities to increase access to high level programming such as distance learning courses and to increase connections to resources outside of the school walls. In implementing services, educators in gifted, general, special education programs, and related professional services collaborate with one another and parents/guardians and community members to ensure that students' diverse learning needs are met. Administrators demonstrate their support of these programming options by allocating sufficient resources so that all students within gifts and talents receive appropriate educational services.

Standard 5: Programming
Description: Educators are aware of empirical evidence regarding (a) the cognitive, creative, and affective development of learners with gifts and talents, and (b) programming that meets their concomitant needs. Educators use this expertise systematically and collaboratively to develop, implement, and effectively manage comprehensive services for students with a variety of gifts and talents to ensure specific student outcomes.

Student Outcomes	**Evidence-Based Practices**
5.1. Variety of Programming. Students with gifts and talents participate in a variety of evidence-based programming options that enhance performance in cognitive and affective areas.	5.1.1. Educators regularly use multiple alternative approaches to accelerate learning. 5.1.2. Educators regularly use enrichment options to extend and deepen learning opportunities within and outside of the school setting. 5.1.3. Educators regularly use multiple forms of grouping, including clusters, resource rooms, special classes, or special schools. 5.1.4. Educators regularly use individualized learning options such as mentorships, internships, online courses, and independent study. 5.1.5. Educators regularly use current technologies, including online learning options and assistive technologies to enhance access to high-level programming. 5.1.6. Administrators demonstrate support for gifted programs through equitable allocation of resources and demonstrated willingness to ensure that learners with gifts and talents receive appropriate educational services.
5.2. Coordinated Services. Students with gifts and talents demonstrate progress as a result of the shared commitment and coordinated services of gifted education, general education, special education, and related professional services, such as school counselors, school psychologists, and social workers.	5.2.1. Educators in gifted, general, and special education programs, as well as those in specialized areas, collaboratively plan, develop, and implement services for learners with gifts and talents.

Student Outcomes	Evidence-Based Practices
5.3. Collaboration. Students with gifts and talents' learning is enhanced by regular collaboration among families, community, and the school.	5.3.1. Educators regularly engage families and community members for planning, programming, evaluating, and advocating.
5.4. Resources. Students with gifts and talents participate in gifted education programming that is adequately funded to meet student needs and program goals.	5.4.1. Administrators track expenditures at the school level to verify appropriate and sufficient funding for gifted programming and services.
5.5. Comprehensiveness. Students with gifts and talents develop their potential through comprehensive, aligned programming and services.	5.5.1. Educators develop thoughtful, multi-year program plans in relevant student talent areas, PK–12.
5.6. Policies and Procedures. Students with gifts and talents participate in regular and gifted education programs that are guided by clear policies and procedures that provide for their advanced learning needs (e.g., early entrance, acceleration, credit in lieu of enrollment).	5.6.1. Educators create policies and procedures to guide and sustain all components of the program, including assessment, identification, acceleration practices, and grouping practices, that is built on an evidence-based foundation in gifted education.
5.7. Career Pathways. Students with gifts and talents identify future career goals and the talent development pathways to reach those goals.	5.7.1. Educators provide professional guidance and counseling for individual student strengths, interests, and values. 5.7.2. Educators facilitate mentorships, internships, and vocational programming experiences that match student interests and aptitudes.

Gifted Education Programming Standard 6: Professional Development

Introduction

Professional development is essential for all educators involved in the development and implementation of gifted programs and services. Professional development is the intentional development of professional expertise as outlined by the NAGC-CEC teacher preparation standards and is an ongoing part of gifted educators' professional and ethical practice. Professional development may take many forms ranging from district-sponsored workshops and courses, university courses, professional conferences, independent studies, and presentations by external consultants and should be based on systematic needs assessments and professional reflection. Students participating in gifted education programs and services are taught by teachers with developed expertise in gifted education. Gifted education program services are developed and supported by administrators, coordinators, curriculum specialists, general education, special education, and gifted education teachers who have developed expertise in gifted education. Since students with gifts and talents spend much of their time within general education classrooms, general education teachers need to receive professional development in gifted education that enables them to recognize the characteristics of giftedness in diverse populations, understand the school or district referral and identification process, and possess an array of high quality, research-based differentiation strategies that challenge students. Services for students with gifts and talents are enhanced by guidance and counseling professionals with expertise in gifted education.

Standard 6: Professional Development

Description: All educators (administrators, teachers, counselors, and other instructional support staff) build their knowledge and skills using the NAGC-CEC Teacher Standards for Gifted and Talented Education and the National Staff Development Standards. They formally assess professional development needs related to the standards, develop and monitor plans, systematically engage in training to meet the identified needs, and demonstrate mastery of standard. They access resources to provide for release time, funding for continuing education, and substitute support. These practices are judged through the assessment of relevant student outcomes.

Student Outcomes	Evidence-Based Practices
6.1. Talent Development. Students develop their talents and gifts as a result of interacting with educators who meet the national teacher preparation standards in gifted education.	6.1.1. Educators systematically participate in ongoing, research-supported professional development that addresses the foundations of gifted education, characteristics of students with gifts and talents, assessment, curriculum planning and instruction, learning environments, and programming. 6.1.2. The school district provides professional development for teachers that models how to develop environments and instructional activities that encourage students to express diverse characteristics and behaviors that are associated with giftedness. 6.1.3. Educators participate in ongoing professional development addressing key issues such as anti-intellectualism and trends in gifted education such as equity and access. 6.1.4. Administrators provide human and material resources needed for professional development in gifted education (e.g. release time, funding for continuing education, substitute support, webinars, or mentors).

Student Outcomes	Evidence-Based Practices
	6.1.5. Educators use their awareness of organizations and publications relevant to gifted education to promote learning for students with gifts and talents.
6.2. Socio-emotional Development. Students with gifts and talents develop socially and emotionally as a result of educators who have participated in professional development aligned with national standards in gifted education and National Staff Development Standards.	6.2.1. Educators participate in ongoing professional development to support the social and emotional needs of students with gifts and talents.
6.3. Lifelong Learners. Students develop their gifts and talents as a result of educators who are life-long learners, participating in ongoing professional development and continuing education opportunities.	6.3.1. Educators assess their instructional practices and continue their education in school district staff development, professional organizations, and higher education settings based on these assessments. 6.3.2. Educators participate in professional development that is sustained over time, that includes regular follow-up, and that seeks evidence of impact on teacher practice and on student learning. 6.3.3. Educators use multiple modes of professional development delivery including online courses, online and electronic communities, face-to-face workshops, professional learning communities, and book talks. 6.3.4. Educators identify and address areas for personal growth for teaching students with gifts and talents in their professional development plans.
6.4. Ethics. Students develop their gifts and talents as a result of educators who are ethical in their practices.	6.4.1. Educators respond to cultural and personal frames of reference when teaching students with gifts and talents. 6.4.2. Educators comply with rules, policies, and standards of ethical practice.

Note. From *NAGC Pre-K–Grade 12 Gifted Programming Standards. A Blueprint for Quality Gifted Education Programs* (pp. 8–13), by National Association for Gifted Children, 2010, Washington, DC: Author. Copyright 2010 by National Association for Gifted Children. Reprinted with permission.

The Association for the Gifted (TAG), a Division of the Council for Exceptional Children, and its Board of Directors have reviewed these standards and express support of the NAGC Pre-K-Grade 12 Programming Standards. April 2010.

About TAG

The Association for the Gifted (TAG) was organized as a division of The Council for Exceptional Children in 1958. TAG plays a major part in helping both professionals and parents work more effectively with one of our most precious resources: the gifted child. Visit http://www.cectag.org for more information.

Appendix B

Decision-Making Strategies

Six Ws

Who	
What	
Where	
When	
Why	
To What Extent	

Hexagonal Radial

Focus, Issues, Factors

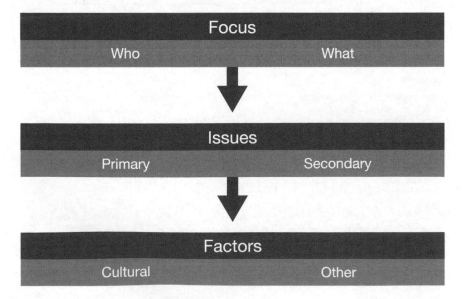

Basic Radial

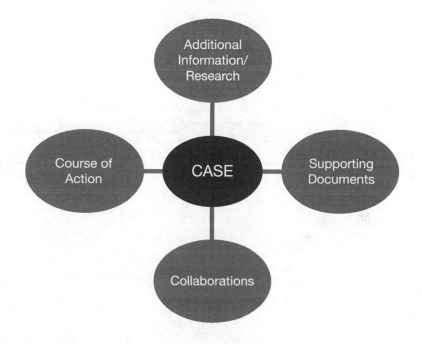

T-Chart

QUESTIONS	RESPONSES

Skillful Problem Solving

SKILLFUL PROBLEM SOLVING

THE PROBLEM

How might I _____?

POSSIBLE SOLUTIONS
How can I solve the problem?

SOLUTION CONSIDERED

CONSEQUENCES What will happen if I adopt this solution?	PRO OR CON?	VALUE How important is the consequence? Why?

NEW SOLUTION
How can the solution be
changed to make it
better?

Skillful Decision Making

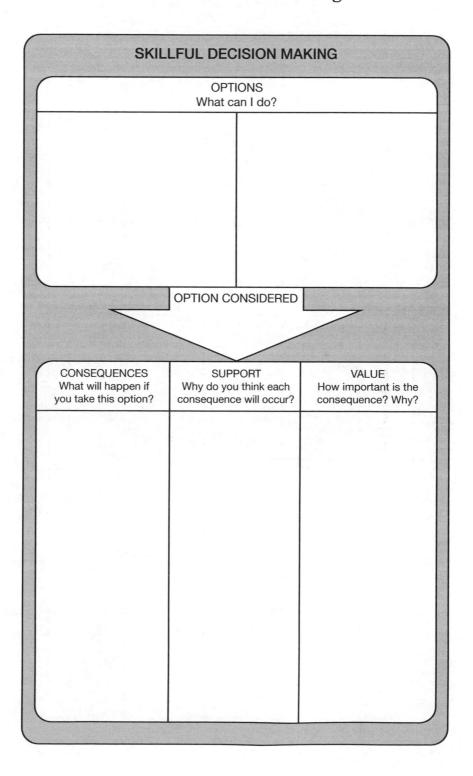

Decision-Making Matrix

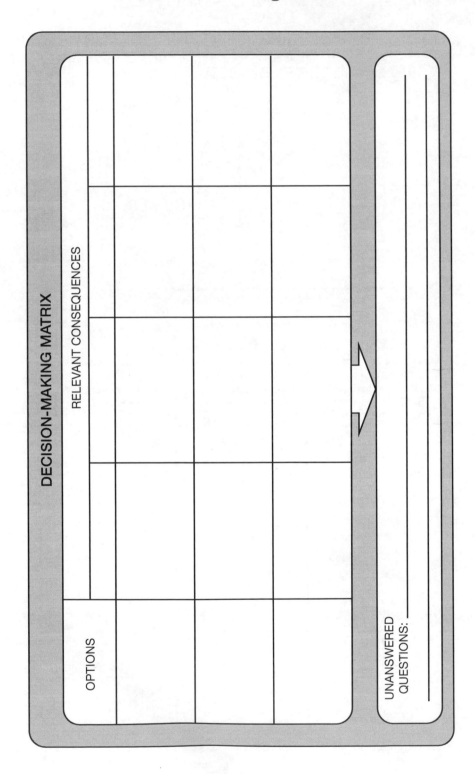

Decision Wheel

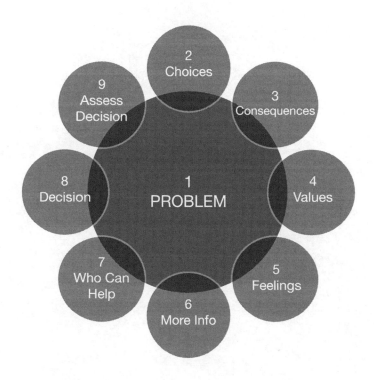

Conflict Solution

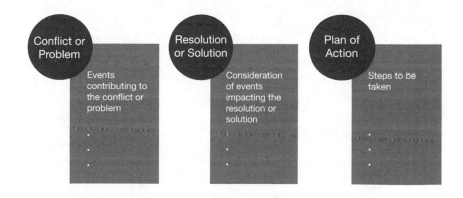

Appendix C

Sample Case With Decision-Making Strategies

Mrs. Tyler and Derek

Introduction

The characteristics of gifted children can lead to social and emotional problems that may affect their emotional and social development. Just because a student is identified as gifted does not mean he or she does everything perfectly, is well-behaved, or emotionally mature. While recognizing there is a relationship between social as well as emotional needs and cognitive needs, support systems in school and at home are needed for guiding the development of a gifted child.

Mrs. Tyler is a first-year language arts teacher assigned to a fifth- and sixth-grade mix of 16 gifted students for half a day, a general education class of 24, and then a remedial class of 12 for the remainder of the day. Mrs. Tyler's coursework included a master's in special education with an emphasis in gifted education. She held several teaching positions as a substitute and taught a number of special programs for gifted learners on Saturdays, as well as during summer. This is her first full-time teaching assignment.

Mrs. Tyler has a fifth-grade student, Derek, who is exhibiting habitually troublesome behaviors in the classroom. One action that she notes is the constant shouting out of the word "eh" throughout the class period, which is distracting not only to Mrs. Tyler but to the other students as well. Whenever Derek makes this noise, the other students laugh. She also notices that Derek has trouble spelling some of the basic words and his handwriting is difficult to read because he likes to write in very tiny print. When Derek does focus, it is on topics he likes; however, he is often off-task for others, especially when asked to complete a writing prompt. He is very artistic and does not like to write unless he is doodling. Mrs. Tyler notes that Derek exhibits some behaviors associated with Attention Deficit/Hyperactivity Disorder (ADHD). He is also well-read, but again, only when the topic is of interest to him. Derek enjoys being the "class clown" and often looks for ways to gain the attention of his classmates with his comments and antics. Derek is tall, gangly, and not at all athletic. He has one male friend in class. The remaining students tend to tolerate him, but do not include him in their conversations and activities beyond the classroom.

Things to Consider

- *Highly gifted children are more susceptible to some types of developmental difficulties than are moderately gifted or average children.*
- *There are outside influences that impact a gifted learner.*
- *Peer approval is important for the adolescent child, especially for the gifted whose interests and abilities may contribute to feelings of isolation.*
- *Some children with strong academic promise fail to perform at levels of achievement that are commensurate with their ability.*

After checking Derek's academic records, Mrs. Tyler discovers his recent IQ score of 146 and his standardized achievement scores range from average to above average. This seemed somewhat surprising to Mrs. Tyler, as she was expecting all scores to be in the above average range. His school grades were mixed, seemingly declining over the past 2 years. Mrs. Tyler wonders if this is a reflection of Derek's ability, time management, lack of interest, or possibly a twice-exceptionality. Derek's file also included the notation that during the previous year Derek had hidden on a school bus, enabling him to sneak off at a later bus stop to cut the telephone cable to his house. He did so to prevent the school from contacting his mother to discuss his poor report card grades. His mother, a single parent and registered nurse working full-time, does not know what to do with him. She is concerned about his future and his influence on his younger brother.

Who—Mrs. Tyler, Derek, and Derek's mother
What—Exhibited troublesome cognitive, social, and emotional behaviors in the classroom
Where—Fifth-grade language arts class
When—During class time
Why—To distract others, gain attention, frustrate the teacher, and avoid classwork
To what extent—Extreme

Figure 13. Derek: Six Ws.

Analyzing the case

For a better analysis of a case, the following decision-making tools are provided. The tools selected for this sample are only a representation of what the reader could use. Other tools may be helpful in processing the facts presented.

It is useful to consider the facts using the Six Ws (see Figure 13) in order to have a better understanding about the case and all of its complex components. The Six Ws can be beneficial in answering many of the questions associated with a case.

To determine the problem(s) and consequences of a possible solution as it relates to a case, one can use the Skillful Problem Solving Organizer (see Appendix B; see Figure 14). The cases purposefully do not include a specific outcome so that the reader can explore many possibilities. Although solving the case is not specifically required in the activities, many readers may find it beneficial to consider major and minor problems as well as to discuss or research various options. In doing so, readers may find this process helpful and applicable to situations or circumstances associated with local school or building issues.

The Skillful Decision Making Organizer (see Appendix B; see Figure 15) is another tool one can use to determine a variety of options once they have identified a problem(s). The consideration of consequences, support, and value add an in-depth dimension for reflection about a case such as Derek's.

The needs of the reader and the nature of the case determine which strategies or tools can assist with analysis and decision making. If time is available, consider what questions, activities, and extensions could be developed for the case.

SKILLFUL PROBLEM SOLVING

THE PROBLEM

How might I _____redirect Derek's social behavior in the classroom_____?

POSSIBLE SOLUTIONS
How can I solve the problem?

I can determine whether this misbehavior might be an underlying result of a disability (e.g., Tourette's Syndrome (TS) or ADHD). If not a disability, I can work with campus special education professionals to do the following:

1. I can determine if there are causes of misbehavior that I can control, such as putting Derek toward the back of the classroom and out of sight from classmates.

2. I can determine if the use of a reinforcement strategy will reduce disruptive behavior, such as giving Derek another option when he feels compelled to say

the word "eh."

3. I can determine if the misbehavior is classroom based.

4. I can use a behavior modification technique.

5. I can teach Derek self-control and self-monitoring strategies.

6. I can determine whether this misbehavior might be a result of curricular and instructional strategies that do not sufficiently meet Derek's needs.

7. I can determine whether this misbehavior might be a result of Derek's inability to understand the concepts taught.

SOLUTION CONSIDERED

I can give Derek another option when he feels compelled to say the word "eh" by providing a popsicle stick with the word written on it.

CONSEQUENCES What will happen if I adopt this solution?	PRO OR CON?	VALUE How important is the consequence? Why?
The other students will not be able to hear or see Derek and thus not be distracted during class, especially if he is placed in the back of the classroom. Behavior may extinguish when Derek does not get the attention he craves.	Pro	Providing the word "eh" on a popsicle stick (that can be raised when the need to say the word is overwhelming) validates Derek's need for attention, but does not disturb his classmates. The teacher can accomplish this with little effort, time, or cost.

NEW SOLUTION
How can the solution be changed to make it better?

I may need to reevaluate if it does not work.

Figure 14. Skillful problem solving for Derek.

SKILLFUL DECISION MAKING

OPTIONS
What can I do?

- I can contact the parent to discuss my concerns and suggest that the parent seek consultation with Derek's healthcare provider.

- I can move Derek's desk to another location in the classroom.

- I can determine if there is another way Derek can say "eh" without disturbing classmates.

- I can provide Derek with a squeeze ball to use

when he is anxious or feels the need to blurt out in class.

- I can have Derek tested by the school psychologist to determine if there are any disorders or learning differences.

- I can meet with the guidance counselor to discuss concerns related to the patterns of underachievement and a possible need for intervention.

OPTION CONSIDERED

I can determine if the use of a reinforcement strategy will reduce disruptive behavior, such as giving Derek another option when he feels compelled to say the word "eh."

CONSEQUENCES What will happen if you take this option?	SUPPORT Why do you think each consequence will occur?	VALUE How important is the consequence? Why?
• I will justify Derek's need to say this word, but do so in a way that does not disturb the class. • Derek may not cooperate and it will not work. • I may have to try various approaches.	• Derek will feel his needs are validated. • Derek does not desire to change his behavior. • This might not be the best approach. Derek may need to determine his own approach.	• Very important because Derek will have an alternative response resulting in a positive experience. • Very important because the problem may escalate. • Very important because it may have me consider other causes and effects of Derek's behavior, or provide an opportunity for him to take more responsibility for his actions.

Figure 15. Skillful decision making for Derek.

About the Authors

Christine L. Weber, Ph.D., is an associate professor of Childhood Education, Literacy, and TESOL at the University of North Florida in Jacksonville. She instructs teachers in strategies for conceptual teaching and learning, assessment tools, and meeting the needs of gifted learners. She has been a member of the Editorial Review Board for *Gifted Child Today* since 1998. Under her leadership, the *Florida's Frameworks for K–12 Gifted Learners* was developed in 2007 and disseminated to all school districts in the state. Weber has published numerous articles and presented at state, national (including National Association of Gifted Children), and international conferences related to the education of gifted children. She currently serves as Secretary for the Florida Association for the Gifted (FLAG). She was awarded the Outstanding Undergraduate Teaching Award from the University of North Florida in 2007.

Cecelia Boswell, Ed.D., has more than 40 years of experience in education. She worked throughout Texas writing online courses and managing a variety of projects for Texas Education Agency and conducting research for the Texas International Baccalaureate Schools. Boswell is a member of the board of the Council for Exceptional Children—The Association for the Gifted and author of the publication on strategies for twice-exceptional gifted children, *Effective Program Practices for Underserved Gifted Students* (with Cheryll Adams). She is also author of *RtI for the Gifted Student* (with Valerie Dodd Carlisle). Boswell is currently the executive director of advanced academic services for Waco Independent School District in Waco, TX, where she has developed a new Middle School Academy for gifted/talented students in grades 6–8.

Wendy Behrens, M.A. Ed., serves as the Gifted and Talented Education Specialist for the Minnesota Department of Education, providing leadership and consultation services for educators, administrators, and parents. She provides technical assistance to and collaborates with institutions of higher education, professional organizations, educator networks, and others interested in promoting rigorous educational opportunities. Prior to her service to the state, Behrens worked for 12 years as a district K–12 gifted services coordinator and a consultant for the Science Museum of Minnesota. She is a frequent presenter on instructional strategies, assessment, comprehensive service design and evaluation, and policies that support gifted education. She has been invited to make presentations on various topics related to the education of gifted and high potential at-risk learners in the Middle East, Far East, and Europe.

She serves on the board of the Council of State Directors of Programs for the Gifted, as Chair of the Development and Fund Raising Committee for the National Association of Gifted Children (NAGC), and is a member of the NAGC Policy Task Force and advisory councils for the Northwestern University Center for Talent Development and the University of St. Thomas.